Kids on the 'Net

Conducting Internet Research in K–5 Classrooms

Jessica G. Morton

Heinemann
Portsmouth, NH

Heinemann
A division of Reed Elsevier Inc.
361 Hanover Street
Portsmouth, NH 03801–3912
http://www.heinemann.com

Offices and agents throughout the world

The author and publisher wish to thank those who have generously given permission to reprint borrowed material.

Library of Congress Cataloging-in-Publication Data
Morton, Jessica G.
Kids on the 'Net : conducting Internet research in K–5 classrooms / Jessica G. Morton.
p. cm.
"Beeline books."
Includes bibliographical references (p. 81).
ISBN 0–325–00021–2
1. Internet (Computer network) in education. 2. Electronic mail systems. I. Title.
LB1044.87.M67 1998
371.33'467'8—dc21 98-26658
CIP

Editor: Amy L. Cohn
Production: Elizabeth Valway
Cover design: Darci Mehall/Aureo Design
Interior design: Greta D. Sibley & Associates
Interior photos: John Birchard and Mark & Jessica Morton
Manufacturing: Louise Richardson

Printed in the United States of America on acid-free paper
02 01 00 99 98 ML 1 2 3 4 5

For Mark and Maggie
Two of my favorite M's.

Contents

Acknowledgments vi

Introduction viii

Chapter 1 *Thinking in a "Connected" Classroom* 1

Chapter 2 *Creating Background Experiences for E-mail Research* 11

Chapter 3 *Choosing a Topic for Long-term Student Research* 23

Chapter 4 *Getting Comfortable with the Internet* 30

Chapter 5 *Getting Started with E-pals and Practicing Good Netiquette* 41

Chapter 6 *Introducing the Concept—and the Correspondents—to Students* 50

Chapter 7 *Strategies to Help Internet Work Run Smoothly* 55

Chapter 8 *Connections, Extensions, and Assessment* 69

Appendices *Observation Form* 77
Some Common Country Codes 78
Some Useful Internet Addresses for Teachers 79

Bibliography 81

Acknowledgments

I would like to thank the following people, in slightly chronological order. I am grateful to each of them for the contributions they made, directly or indirectly, to this book.

Ken Matheson, our remarkable superintendent, and Mitch Sprague, a very knowledgeable and supportive teacher, made the first "Bringing Curriculum Alive" summer workshop appealing and useful. They continue to actively support teachers in assisted risk taking. I'm grateful to Andrea McCurdy, who worked with the Autodesk Foundation and NASA to bring the Internet to every classroom in our school district, and to Pacific Bell's Education First project, for supporting and encouraging our district to take technological leaps. Jodi Reed has been part of that great group, and made suggestions for some of the URLs in the Appendix. The Autodesk Foundation itself has also provided valuable, ongoing support to our district. In addition, their annual Project-Based Learning conferences encourage deliberate, inspired teaching with technology.

I am deeply grateful to every informed correspondent whose generosity with their time, expertise, and enthusiasm made our classroom e-mail research possible. I am fortunate to have known each of the children who voiced their interesting questions and were pleased by our correspondents' delightful answers. Amanda Lutz and Kristin Otwell made sending e-mail feasible that first year, when they worked as outstanding aides—and much more—in our classroom.

Elizabeth Share of Autodesk has been a writer's perfect friend, graciously reading and helping to refine the manuscript and encouraging me through the bumpy spots. Rich Lundy, my high school English teacher, picked up his red pen once again to carefully check an early draft of the manuscript. He continues to help me enjoy literacy every time I receive one of his e-mails. Jan Johnson has been a devoted e-pal and colleague, one of the best friends I've never met.

Two people kindly gave me their immediate assistance with valuable resources: Rennie Innis of Mendocino Community Network shared his favorite introductory Internet books, and Rudie Tretten of Saint Mary's College talked with me about his assessment research for the Autodesk Foundation.

My daughter Maggie typed the bibliography and, as a writer herself, always understood if I was mid-sentence and couldn't be interrupted or if I needed a break!

My parents, Jess and Helen Gresett, are new Internet users in their 80s, and deserve mention here for learning to send e-mail to me. Leigh Peake at Heinemann first believed my idea sounded like a Heinemann book, and has been a warm and helpful presence in bringing it to light as has Elizabeth Valway in production. And most of all, thanks, Mark, for nudging me to write a book about this, and then helping every step of the way.

Introduction

The computer beeps. Children look up briefly from their work; someone announces, "E-mail!" and two students walk over to the computer. They click the mouse, watch the screen, and turn toward me. "It's from Peter and Billie Ann!" they tell us, and prepare to print out two copies of the letter our class has just received. These friends in Vienna, Austria, have just returned from a birding vacation in Botswana, where they mailed the children two postcards we've already received. The two children walk down the hall to the printer in the office, then return a few moments later with the printed letter in hand, ready to learn more about this couple's trip to Africa and the birds they saw while there.

Each year, my students and I share our classroom with five to fifteen experts in the topic we're studying. These people come to us from as far away as Finland and Australia, and provide us with instant answers to the questions the children continually raise about our topic for the year. Some of our informed helpers are university professors, others are graduate students, and some are birding hobbyists or work as volunteers in bird rehabilitation or nature centers. They manage to enthusiastically juggle the responsibilities of their jobs, families, and hobbies along with the questions we ask daily. They take up no space in our classroom and the only sound they make is an occasional beep in the corner when our computer announces the arrival of new mail.

Sharing books on the year-long topic creates connections as well as prompting student questions.

These people have all agreed to be our research helpers for the year, via e-mail. Here are some of the many benefits of their presence in our classroom:

- We can invite children to wonder and to ask as many questions as they want, as often as they like.
- Our correspondents and I can honor this invitation to be curious daily, and thereby provide children with the delight inherent in spontaneous, ongoing, focused inquiry.
- We can challenge young children to explore a single topic, immersed to an extent usually reserved for much older students.
- We can assure them that every question will be treated with respect, and every query will be sent to someone likely to know how to answer it.
- We can converse with informed people almost anywhere in the world, learning *from* them as well as *about* them.

First- and second-graders in my class have, for the past four years, experienced all this and more—through the power of the Internet.

I hadn't even heard of the Internet five years ago. When I began our classroom e-mail research project, I had barely used e-mail or other online resources myself. It was a huge leap for this beginner to decide to introduce such new technology into the classroom. My Internet training at the time consisted of a week-long class in our district's computer lab during the summer. That class, combined with solid peer and administrative support, encouraged me to take the challenge to use the Internet with young children. I took some comfort in basing our work on a topic I had successfully taught several times: birds.

The untested part of the experiment that first year—bringing informed strangers into our classroom via computer—took us far beyond the scope of any previous study of birds in my class. My initial idea for using the Internet with students was simply to support our existing unit on birds, enlisting the aid of a few bird experts as backup information sources. I had no idea when we began that our attitudes about learning itself would be so deeply, positively, and permanently affected.

Because the children knew the experts were there, waiting like wise grandparents with plenty of time, knowledge, and patience, they began to change. Students began arriving at school eager to share their bird sightings, observations, and questions. It was no longer a rare experience for them to go beyond the books we read and experiences we had in class and on hikes; it became the norm. This was because the children knew there were people always available, ready to answer whatever they wondered about. The vocabulary introduced by our e-pals was far richer and more complex than anything I had taught such young children. Impressive big new words such as *precocial* and *altricial*, *iridescent* and *understory*, entered our classroom, carrying meaning and power. Because they were presented in the context of personal answers to the children's own questions, and gave the children the status of fellow scientists, these complex words were remembered and used by the class!

Jessica,

I thought I would drop you a line to see how your study of birds was going. I shared your last post with some colleagues and they were very impressed with the questions and the *vocabulary*.

I had the opportunity to go to a 3rd grade classroom the other day to dissect cow eyes with them. The reason I was so willing to go was because of the experience I've had with your class.

Thanks for showing me how inquisitive and interesting elementary students can be. Let me know if I can help your class in the future.

Thanks.
Jack

Our expert Internet helpers have all been adults, with the exception of one student who first joined us as a sixth-grader. They live as far away as Australia, Finland, and Hong Kong, but through months of interaction and shared thinking, we came to feel they were as close as the class next door. I was able to find these wise and patient people by creatively searching, observing, and eventually sending requests for their help by e-mail. We were able to stay connected by sending questions and by being considerate, appreciative correspondents.

I've written this book to share the learning magic that happens when children can spontaneously talk to—and be responded to by—experts on rich topics that involve and interest them both. My goal is to explain, as simply and clearly as I can, the mechanics of reaching out to the world by using a computer and a network connection, and to tell some stories about our experiences when my students and I became connected to that larger world.

None of us can predict precisely where we'll arrive when children's authentic questions—and the answers they generate—help guide our curriculum. I find energy, excitement, and ownership in this new form of student-guided research: children actively learning about what matters to them, in the company of people graciously sharing their extensive knowledge and passion for the subject. This approach lets you and your students stroll freely where curiosity leads, supported by informed experts who know a great deal about where you're wandering and how to find some of the most interesting paths. I hope this book can help you open your own classroom to the magic that is out there!

Chapter 1

Thinking in a "Connected" Classroom

My students and I have just finished reading about swallows' nests in a book entitled *And So They Build* (Kitchen). The children are amazed to learn that these birds must fill their beaks with mud approximately a thousand times to complete a single nest. I remember reading elsewhere that if swallows build a nest where mud isn't available, they fly to a water source, fill their beaks there, and fly back to the nesting site in order to make their own mud. I describe this and Connor asks, "Why don't they just use their saliva?" Since birds don't have teeth and we've learned they don't chew their food, I suggest they may have different saliva production than we do. "Do birds even have saliva?" someone else asks. "That sounds like a good research question for writing time," I say, hoping someone will choose to send the question about birds and their saliva to one of our waiting bird experts.

In my classroom, I have a computer that is connected to the Internet, and it is this connection that allows me to finally follow through on one of the beliefs I had as a beginning teacher: I wanted to allow time and space for children's questions, because they're supremely worth listening to and pursuing. There was, I had sadly discovered, a huge and often impassable gap between respecting my students' innate curiosity and actively supporting it. In previous years, I had found the sheer number and variety of their questions overwhelming. I often ran out of time, patience, and answers much too quickly.

In 1993, I took a week-long summer class taught by one of my colleagues which led, quite accidentally, to a solution to this conflict. The class had been planned to help teachers learn about resources on the Internet; we were expected to emerge able to write curriculum that would encourage wider student and teacher use of this new technology in schools. The goals were to make us less timid about using online resources, to have us venture beyond packaged, commercial computer programs or simulations, and to create useful lessons for other teachers that integrated technology with curriculum. Having blazed this electronic trail, we could lead other teachers to actively use the Internet in their own classrooms.

In the class, we were guided daily through different parts of what then existed on the Internet. The instructor lectured each morning, and the afternoons were free for individual exploration. It was a model of innovation based on attraction rather than coercion, and it worked. When, on day three, I finally found newsgroups—online discussion groups organized around specific topics—I felt I'd found a very valuable hidden treasure, though I wasn't yet sure just what to do with it.

I'd been stubbornly, proudly resistant to the idea of young children using computers. I believed, and still do, that young children do their best learning through direct experience. They make sense of the world through repeated experiences that have meaning for them personally. However, I have come to believe that we can't ignore the power and usefulness of computers: We simply must choose to be in charge of humanizing the technology.

For my work in the summer course, I wanted to somehow augment my year-long birds curriculum unit by using the Internet; I was not at all sure how I would accomplish this. To learn what online resources were available, I first visited some websites about birds. At that point, any bird information I was able to find was usually at a library web site. Everything I found was dry, technical, and academic. The text was tiny. There was no color, no sound. Pictures that were occasionally available to download took several minutes to fill my screen. I could have more efficiently and productively driven to our local library and checked out a few books on birds for my young students.

It was easy to see that those "electronic book page" sites weren't going to do much to inspire or enrich my combined first and second grade class. Things have changed dramatically since then. It's now possible for anyone with the time and interest to view beautiful and informative web pages that download fairly quickly, even with highly detailed color, art, and sound. Fortunately, the very limitations I found when searching the Web for resources for my students are what serendipitously led me to the project, and to the concept I describe in this book.

Halfway through the class, we were shown newsgroups. These forums intrigued me. Here was something on the Internet neither boring nor lifeless. Finally, something immediate: Here was a resource where people with similar interests met and communicated, electronically. And—a surprise gift for my curriculum project—many of them were using a news group called "rec.birds" and having a great time sharing information on our topic!

Suddenly, a completely new direction seemed possible for my birds project. I imagined my students writing directly to people who were interested in birds, and, better yet, dared hope that these birders would provide personalized answers to my students' questions. I decided to have the children write to individuals I selected ahead of time, rather than posting their questions to entire newsgroups. This was a naive but very fortunate choice on my part, and it influenced the personalized quality of our correspondence far beyond what I could have envisioned when we began.

I excitedly posted my first message about the proposed project on a few appropriate newsgroups and waited, not at all sure what would happen. (See Appendix for a list of some useful newsgroup listings for teachers). I didn't have to wait long; within minutes, I was rewarded with the first of many enthusiastic, intriguing replies from birders who had read my message and wanted to help us. From these answers, I eventually chose the most articulate and interested-sounding writers to become the children's correspondents during the school year and beyond. I was elated: The project had already begun to take shape!

During the next school year, and each year after, my students had genuine and mutually enjoyable conversations with people who shared their interests and honored their questions. They are conversations, not abrupt question-and-answer sessions, because collegial relationships were built during the course of each year between my students and our e-mail helpers. The children's research came alive, nurtured in a context that involved people who were interested in my students and their ideas as well as their questions.

And the small-town world my students inhabit enlarged immeasurably in the capable hands of these experts.

Several aspects of this "correspondence learning" led me to let go—at least a little!—of the need to feel in control of so much of what I used to do in our class. This has been a long-term struggle for me as a teacher, between ideals and pragmatism, efficiency and spontaneity. Now, instead of my agenda, it has become the children's as well. Their own questions drive much of our science curriculum. Our e-mail correspondents help the children develop an increased disposition to question, consider, hypothesize, and evaluate. As students interpret and talk about the replies they receive, they formulate new questions, and each new question guides us in surprising and rewarding ways to our next step in learning.

People with field experience, as well as those with theoretical knowledge, people with time as well as interest in our topic, have become part of daily life in our classroom. Not everyone has answers at hand for us; some simply tell us we have stumped them, while others ask colleagues or do research themselves. And others may even suggest that we test their information and impress our friends:

Three of our weekly "computer experts" check for recent e-mail.

Dear John,

Connor is wondering what their temperature is when birds puff up. He thinks the temperature is a lot hotter than it is before the birds puff up, because they do it in the winter and they stay pretty warm. Thanks for your help. Connor

Connor is absolutely right. Puffed up feathers make one of the best insulators (which is just a fancy word for something that keeps you warm) there is. . . .

I just thought of one more thing that birds use puffed-up feathers for: helping them float. Right now there are a lot of grebes swimming on the ocean where I live (and probably where you live, too, though maybe today wouldn't be the best day to go look at them, what with all this rain, huh?), and if you watch a grebe closely while it's swimming around you'll see something very interesting.

When the grebe is paddling along on top of the water its feathers are fluffed way out, and it floats really high. When the grebe is getting ready to dive under the water, though, (which it does to look for fish to eat or to get away from things that scare it), its feathers flatten way down, and the grebe starts to sink into the water. With all the air pushed out of its feathers, the grebe can dive really easily. When you know this you can tell what a grebe is about to do just by looking at whether its feathers are puffed out or not.

Impress your friends! Say, "That grebe is about to dive under the water," and a second or two later it will. Your friends will think you have magical powers!

Great question, Connor.

And a great, entertaining, informatively divergent answer from John!

Though each e-mail reply was a gift to the class, some correspondents sent tangible presents as well. We were sent a beautiful photo album of local birds, the pictures taken by e-pals then living in Florida, just to show the children what their local birds were—and we were surprised to see so many familiar birds; because we live on the coast, many of the same birds live here as well. When we received the postcards from European birders vacationing in Botswana, my students were able to identify the carmine bee-eaters on one of the cards: They were the same birds pictured in the magical book *Mufaro's Beautiful Daughters*, which we were reading when the card arrived!

Because so much teaching and learning now comes from these skilled adults outside our class, I am able to step back and enjoy the children's experiences, to watch this lively new learning process unfold. Best of all, there are ideas, attitudes, and fascinating information far beyond my own expertise that are now entering our classroom from the world beyond. While it enriches us and demonstrates the power and delight of young children being heard and taken seriously as thinkers and scientists, the e-mail is gratifying on a simpler level, too—we get lots of mail every day.

We are often presented with deep and considered answers to our questions. Even a child's letter that had seemed to require a one-sentence reply grew to encompass a response full of rich vocabulary and complex ideas:

> Dear Mr. Callender,
>
> How long do birds sit on their eggs?
>
> Petra

> Dear Petra,
>
> That's a very good question. The answer is, different birds sit on their eggs for different amounts of time. . . .
>
> People who study birds have noticed an interesting thing about these numbers: birds that spend less time sitting on their eggs have babies that are ugly little helpless things when they first hatch out.

These babies (which bird experts call "altricial") have to spend a relatively long time in the nest while the parent birds bring them food. Baby robins, for example, can't leave the nest until about 15 days after they hatch.

Birds that spend longer sitting on their eggs produce babies that are much more fully formed when they hatch out. (Bird experts call these cute little babies "precocial"). Baby chickens and ducks and ostriches, for examples, can leave the nest almost immediately after hatching.

The children were frequently told by our correspondents, "That's a really hard question!" or "You have asked something scientists are still arguing about," sometimes even before the answer was offered. The children, of course, were delighted to be told that their brains were working so well!

We are also lucky enough to occasionally receive conflicting answers from different respondents. There was a long and unresolved debate among several of our helpers about the terms *bill* and *beak* and whether they were or were not the same. Some people we asked contended that only hooked eating equipment qualifies as a beak (such as that found on parrots and eagles) and any other shapes (such as those found on robins, sparrows, and ducks) are bills; other writers told the children that the two words were completely interchangeable.

The children were fascinated by this discussion, and several others that were similarly open-ended. Like a game missing the instructions, it is far more intriguing to them to have an answer left open than any simple and final fact would have been. These conflicting answers often lead to more questions and deeper thinking among my students. The contrast with my earlier classroom discussion style is dramatic: Rather than the "dead end" we create when we answer a child's question efficiently and narrowly, we've learned to enjoy these contradictory responses as a sign that we've asked something truly difficult, even for scientists, to answer.

We were also treated to the courtesy of being asked for our own theories and ideas by one of our correspondents. John ended his answer to

Petra about how long birds sit on their nests by writing, "I'm curious what you think about why some birds have altricial babies and other birds have precocial babies. Maybe you could e-mail me some of your ideas, Petra. I'd be very interested in reading them." His invitation and interest in learning the children's theories led me to permanently change how we phrase our questions.

One of the most important things I've learned through this project is that e-mail is an ideal vehicle for student inquiry, because of the way it allows for timely yet polite and nonintrusive communication. It's both discreet and instantaneous, more considerate than a phone call, more instant even than overnight mail! Here's how it works:

- We send a note to someone.
- It arrives within moments of being sent.
- The recipient reads it when it's most convenient for her.
- She answers when she has the time to reflect and write back.
- She sends her reply to us when it's most convenient for her.
- We are delighted to read it within moments of its being sent to us.

There are no envelopes to address, no stamps to attach, no mysterious postage to calculate for other countries. And it's so wonderfully fast, we can ask for immediate clarification or more details from our helpers, while student interest remains high and current. And, in case you are still interested in that question about bird saliva, it did get sent—by another student. Here's part of the astounding answer it generated:

> Hi Rigel, you asked if birds have saliva? The answer is yes. . . . Since birds don't have teeth, they can't chew. They can only swallow. Saliva helps them do that. . . . Swifts and some swallows use their saliva to build their nests. There are 71 different species of swifts around the world. During the nest building season, these birds have enlarged salivary glands. . . . Swifts gather twigs, feathers, seeds, grasses, straw, etc. and use their saliva to bind the materials together into a nest, and, depending on where the nest is

located, they also use their saliva to glue the nest in place. The palm swifts, who brood their eggs while clinging vertically to their nest, also use their saliva to "glue" their eggs into the nest for safe-keeping while brooding. Amongst the 71 species of swifts are some swiftlet specie (genus Collocalia) who congregate by the hundreds of thousands in caves in Asia. Some of these species of swiflets build their whole nests from dried saliva and attach them to the roofs or walls of the caves. These are the nests used for the oriental specialty called Bird's Nest Soup. . . . As for the swallows, the two species that build nests here in Austria depend on mud. They cannot use their saliva to make mud. They rely on rain puddles, creeks, small ponds or even the mud you make when you water your lawn. I suspect though that their saliva helps the mud stick together.

These letters demonstrate that my students are responded to as peers in the scientific community, not as pesky little kids with too many questions. The children in our class are almost never talked down to by these e-mail helpers, a pleasant surprise for me and a pleasure for them. There's the same respect and depth of response in letters to children with learning problems, or to those who tend to move at a different pace from others. These children blossom when they feel like powerful communicators. You may have seen the classic "New Yorker" cartoon, which shows two dogs, one typing at a computer keyboard and saying to the other, "On the Internet, no one knows you're a dog." And no one knows, until you tell them, that you're a special education student or a differently abled learner when you're using the Internet, either.

Students who feel less authority and comfort at school are very responsive to a medium that gives them power to communicate this way. They receive enthusiastic responses to their questions like the rest of their classmates, even if they speak slowly or ordinarily have a hard time thinking of the right words. It's especially thrilling to be told that she has come up with a hard question, when school itself is difficult for a child. It's wonderful to see children being given the respect and attention of a personal reply to their thoughts and wonderings, particularly when a permanent copy of that letter can verify to them—as well as to classmates and family—that their thinking was important to someone else.

Through our e-mail research, we are continually shown into the privileged, significant, and fascinating back rooms of scientific inquiry and thought, places usually reserved for graduate students and adult researchers. Many of our most considerate and entertaining hosts have been those graduate students themselves. I think it's no coincidence that we're usually given such excellent, clear, and helpful answers by people who are still learning as an occupation.

Our correspondents share with the children some of the most important and least-discussed secrets of actively learning adulthood, among these:

- The lucky grown-ups among us never get too old to enjoy asking or answering questions.
- Through learning, there are always new pleasures and connections to be discovered in our world.
- Sharing what you know with others and listening well to others make the world a better and friendlier place.
- Finding "The Answer" sometimes isn't the final goal after all. Often, the shared and supported deep wondering creates the real joy, the real accomplishment, in our project.

Chapter 2

Creating Background Experiences for E-mail Research

It's my hope that you'll use this chapter as a springboard for your students' and your curricular interests and needs, and not see it as a recipe to follow precisely. It's here to help give you an insider's view of how our classroom and field experiences work together to shape and stimulate our e-mail research throughout the year. When you and your students begin your own project, please use what's fresh in your region at this time of year, make substitutions freely, and add seasoning to taste.

The curriculum I've created about birds has evolved over many years. What we do in class grows as much as possible from my interest and experiences with the topic and those of my students. We study birds because I'm passionate about them, and because I've seen how bird research captures the attention of my students over an extended period. They're involved in the topic for months, which gives them opportunities to use a very broad range of resources while they're learning. Our e-mail helpers are foremost among these resources.

As teachers, we know we can't make the best use of a guest speaker in our classroom if students have no background on the speaker or her topic. The same is true of online experts. For students to most effectively (and enjoyably) work with these informed people, they first need a common language and experiences that will help them connect well, both with the subject and the experts. For good questions to develop throughout the year, students must be provided with ongoing and engaging experiences and the time to talk about them together. Here is a summary of how we think about birds in our classroom for a year, and how e-mail questions arise from the many ways we experience the topic.

In our classroom, I often set the stage for in-depth study with a collection of books about our area of focus. These books are displayed as a group, read aloud to the class, discussed and compared with each other, reread by individual children, gazed at for their pictures, and used to teach and understand the difference between fiction and nonfiction.

We read many of these books during class story time. Quentin Blake's absurd *Cockatoos* (1992) is even more enjoyable if we can have a real cockatoo come visit class afterwards, to observe and draw it in detail. The highly informative *Urban Roosts: Where Birds Nest in the City* (Barbara Bash, 1990) vividly shows children the adaptations many different birds have made to live successfully in our cities.

Much of the shared reading in our class is either fiction or nonfiction on the year's topic.

I like to read books slowly to children, and will often take several days to read even a simple picture book. I want my students to have time to digest new concepts and vocabulary along with the story. Children who have listened to a book over several days' time can recall that book and its information more easily, even months later, than a book that is consumed at one sitting.

There is a science storage and display center in our room, built by a student's father and the class several years ago. This unit houses a library of reference books and science tools such as magnifiers and balance scales, which are stored on several shelves. We use the large top surface as a display area; here we keep our topic-books collection and all the treasures the children and I bring in to share during the year.

We use the Naturescope Resource book, *Birds, Birds, Birds!* (National Wildlife Federation). It provides good background information for teachers, as well as many activities that help children improve both their observation skills and appreciation of birds.

I've received many nests and feathers over the years. These are displayed and discussed in the first weeks of school, and we spend time on the legal and moral issues that pertain to nature collecting. I try to help children understand that some species of birds will reuse the same nest from year to year, and other birds have evolved needing to use the nest of a previous tenant rather than being able to build their own. Bits of eggshells found on forest walks are added to the collection, and stories, both true and imagined, grow from these objects on our Science Table.

Direct experience is a compelling way to acquire, as well as test, knowledge, and so we go on lots of hikes when we're studying birds and other natural history topics. We visit a variety of different habitats, ranging from the woods next to our school to local beaches. We bring binoculars and field guides, and I try to arrange to have experienced birders or other experts come with us. Hiking with live experts ensures that we'll be able to correctly identify what we notice along the way, and it helps my students better appreciate the knowledge and accessibility that our online experts offer.

On most of our walks, the children have a specific observation form to complete, which I've prepared for the locale we'll be visiting. The form is a bit like a treasure hunt. I use it to encourage children to "collect" birds, trees, other vegetation, or creatures we will likely see and that I want them to notice. Small groups of two to four children usually work together sharing a pencil, clipboard, and observation sheet, but sometimes each hiker is responsible for completing her own form. During the hike, we'll stop periodically to make notes or notice something together.

We bring field guides, and they're used enthusiastically by children, especially when the adults on the hike help the children take responsibility for what they notice. Our class reference collection includes several field guides and commercially laminated quick field identification cards. The children practice using these as often as possible when identifying birds and other interesting things we see. This leads us naturally to the importance of close observation: Looking carefully, and remembering distinguishing marks or other features and attributes, help children identify and thus learn more about what they see in the field.

Repeated trips to the same location are very valuable in a number of ways. Children can see seasonal changes in the same area when allowed to revisit places. A sense of connection grows with a sense of familiarity. Details and subtleties can reveal themselves more easily over time than they do on first sight. Field trip skills (paying attention, and standing perfectly still, at least occasionally) develop when children are accustomed to being outside for focused learning, and not just for recess.

Guest speakers come to our classroom—even guest pets, when possible! The speakers might work in our local parks or pet stores or as bird rehabilitators. Children can practice asking questions of these local experts. They can observe and sketch tame birds at close range, which leads to more learning and wondering about the intriguing variety of physical adaptations among birds. Bill shape, feet and claws, wing shape, all suit each bird to its normal habitat and food sources. We draw and write about these on a recording sheet adapted from Ellen Doris' useful book, *Doing What Scientists Do* (Heinemann).

We usually complete one or more of these observations each month. I collect them during the school year and file them in student folders. This creates a science notebook for each child, which can be referred to throughout the year. At year's end, students can clearly see the progress they've made in their drawing and writing.

We keep a bin of birdseed by the door so children can take turns feeding the birds right outside our windows; this lets us enjoy seeing white-crowned

Name of scientist EMMA Date 2-2-91

I looked at candled eggs

FOOT

What I noticed: I saw a foot. in egg 26. This is 1 of my eggs. I'm icitede beckae I Think 1 of my eggs are going tow hatch.

Open-ended observation sheets can allow for very personal student note-taking and sketching.

Name of scientist EMMa Date 5-6-97

I looked at eggs

What I noticed: The ChickS

peep is very very Qyiite.

These sheets also help focus students' observations, and provide a year-long record of learning.

sparrows and the amiable dark-eyed juncos at close range. Quite a few scavenger birds visit our school daily: Ravens and gulls come to glean crumbs on our playground from the lunches eaten outside. And we're planning a native plants garden to provide cover as well as food that may attract birds to venture closer to our classroom.

Children enthusiastically use the CD ROM *The Multimedia Bird Book* (Workman/Swifte) and the Dorling-Kindersley CD ROM *Birds*. We listen to taped birdcalls and songs (I use "Bird Songs of California," produced by Thomas G. Sander, Wilderness Recordings) as I share facts or ways to identify the birds we're hearing. The children draw diagrams to show the "shape" of the birdcall or song. These visible, personal interpretations help children recall each bird's call or song, and my students eagerly take the test I give on these vocalizations toward the end of our study. Children also make notes about the birds we learn to recognize by sound, to help them remember what's most interesting to them about each one. Their pages become another bird book, and a record of their learning. Videotapes like Dorling-Kindersley's *Birds* and laser discs can show children exotic species, behaviors, and habitats, as well as those they're more familiar with.

Depending on the group I'm working with, some years the children choose topics for extended research projects. They can work in teams or on their own. These projects are a chance for children to choose among and use many resources to support their research, and to present a report to the class on their findings.

In the spring, we incubate chicken eggs. Once, many years ago, we even incubated duck eggs along with the usual chickens. Ducklings are the manic toddlers of the bird world: incredibly cute, far brighter than the average chicken, and experts on making messes. For ducks to eat, their food has to be in water. For my class to survive, I had to clean the ducklings' tiny wading pool several times a day after they gleefully paraded through it, sloshing food, water, and other goodies with abandon. I now limit our incubation to chicken eggs. Unfortunately, a classroom is only so large and a teaching day only so long.

Incubators can vary in quality as much as most machines do: Some are cheap and work only when conditions are perfect; others are more complex and less chancy. We are fortunate enough to be able to borrow the

Mercedes of incubators: the Roll-X. This machine regulates humidity and temperature, and rotates the eggs mechanically. Without a machine this sophisticated, you will gain new respect for birds who do all this for themselves—especially when you have to visit your classroom each weekend during incubation, in order to turn the eggs at regular intervals to prevent the yolks from sticking to one side of the shell.

Where do our eggs come from? We begin by asking students whose families have chickens to donate eggs from home that they suspect might be fertile. We've also incubated fertile, organic grocery store eggs, but with very mixed results. A recent, especially high failure rate of these eggs led us to some of our most urgent and poignant questions: What happened? Why did so few of these "store eggs" mature and hatch out? We used e-mail to explore this problem and were offered several possibilities to consider. One was that when eggs are kept cold (i.e., refrigerated) for an extended time, their viability is compromised. We also learned that the feed used for commercial egg production can be quite different from that used by a family lovingly raising their own chickens outdoors, and so affects egg viability. We were told that the humidity as well as the temperature of the incubator can be off by very small amounts and affect the hatch rate, and that fluctuations in these can harm the developing chick.

I first bring in and crack open a few infertile eggs, so that the children can see the parts and learn their functions. They look carefully, draw them in detail, and write what they notice about the structure and parts of a no longer mundane egg. We refer to our books for the terminology and spelling we need, and the children enjoy making scientific drawings, complete with arrows connecting labels to each part.

The incubation project allows us to integrate math easily into our science. We weigh each egg several times a week in our balance scale, using lightweight math manipulatives that the children choose. Because they have all used interlocking cubes or counting bears, comparing the weight of an egg with these units of measure has real meaning for my young students.

I write a number in pencil on each of the eggs so we can keep track of each one over time. We make a chart containing all of the eggs' numbers, and children record the weight of the eggs each time we weigh them. And they can observe the secret progress inside each egg, because we have the use of an egg candler. This is a large can with a light bulb attached in one end, and a small hole opposite that end against which the egg is held to see inside it.

To candle, we put a few eggs at a time into an egg carton, then wrap it with a towel to maintain warmth while away from the incubator. We find a dark room somewhere in the school and shut the door, eager to see what's going on inside those eggs. When eggs are held against the candler's bright light, we can see through the shells into the mystery hidden inside each egg. At the beginning, all we can see is which eggs have solid-looking yolks and which yolks are almost transparent; the eggs with clear yolks won't develop into chicks. After just a few days in the incubator, the fertile eggs begin to show a distinct eye-spot, and every child in that dark room—and their teacher, too—feels the thrill of a new life beginning right in front of their eyes.

We record this exciting data on the chart, too, and I draw lightly in pencil right on the eggshell what we've seen, tracing the eyespot—and the veins that develop over the next few weeks—so we can later compare for size and location. I also write the date and student-invented codes for our observations on each shell. The children suggest I draw things like a smile, or write the words *yes!*, *eye spot*, and even *movement!*, depending on what they've seen during that observation. The eggs that look ambiguous to us get a question mark written on them. I carefully trace the expanding air sac at the blunt end of each egg. We learn by observing that a fresh egg has almost no air space at the end. An older one has more—a handy way to judge how old your hard-boiled egg is!

We also keep a class Chick Diary. This is a record of the children's observations, theories, and hopes about the eggs as they develop into chicks (or fail to develop). We write these entries as a group, and collect the series to be read later in our class library.

While we're still waiting for the chicks to hatch, I like to read Randall Jarrell's *The Bat-Poet* (1967) for its unusual word-portraits of different bird behaviors and its subtle but effective lessons about the power of poetry. After we've read this book, several students usually want to write poems to and about the chicks, even before they've hatched. Other bird-inspired art has included paintings, drawing, and sculpting. We've also formed nests using natural materials, and then made papier-mâché eggs to put inside them. We carefully paint these after consulting photographs showing the huge variety of egg colors and markings.

I save the incubating and hatching experience for the end of the school year. In spring, once they're old enough to leave the warming light and our classroom, the chickens can safely live outside at children's homes. It works well as a culminating activity, because it allows the children to use and apply what they've learned all year about birds to these "personal birds" in our own classroom.

After hatching, we keep the chicks in the class for several weeks, in a huge cardboard box (such as one from an appliance store) lined thickly with newspaper, which I change daily (or more often). We clip a low-wattage bulb a few inches from the floor of the box, and the baby birds huddle under it whenever they need to get warm. The other equipment is a long metal hopper for the chicks' food and a self-filling water bottle, both bought at a local feed store. We take the birds out as often as possible, and my students find that the birds grow quite tame with gentle and regular handling. Children who have followed the developing chicks from eyespot stage to hatchling understandably feel very connected to these birds. We can observe the chicks at our meeting circle, and see them peck instinctively at the dots on newspaper we've spread on the rug. We can watch the birds' adult feathers growing in, enjoy their first clumsy attempts at flying, and, some years, they even stay long enough so we get to hear rooster try-outs as they perch on every available surface.

We take the chicks out to weigh them in our hopper balance scale. Children are amazed to see how quickly the birds gain weight, and are delighted at how funny a chick looks walking around in the same hopper that recently held it inside its egg. We continue to use the math manipulatives as our unit of measure, and we sometimes make graphs to show weight gain by making stacks of the interlocking cubes themselves to compare from one time to the next, or one bird to another.

Each of these experiences is likely to generate many student questions. To effectively connect the e-mail research to these class experiences, I try to provide plenty of time for children to think and talk about our activities and what we're learning. This kind of reflection time prompts significant questions that children are eager to share with our waiting e-mail correspondents.

Here are some of the questions that students asked our helpers between October 1994 and June 1995. You can find these questions, and their answers, at our bird research website: www.mcn.org/ed/cur/liv/ind/birds.

Eyes, Teeth, Beaks, and Bills

Do birds have different colored eyes like we do?

Do birds have teeth?

What's a bill? What's a beak?

Do toucans have bills or beaks?

How do beaks work?

Nests

How do birds make nests?

Feet and Feathers

Do baby blackbirds have different colored feet than adult blackbirds?

How do birds get their feathers?

Are brightly colored birds poisonous?

How do hummingbirds change their colors in the fog?

Flight

How do birds fly?

How many birds can't fly, and why?

Eggs

Do birds eat eggs?

How long do birds sit on their eggs?

Why are some birds altricial and other birds are precocial?

Are great blue herons altricial or precocial?

Why do birds lay eggs instead of having babies like we do?

Behavior

Do bald eagles fly in herds?

Do birds go to North America from somewhere else?

Do birds go around people?

Do birds eat other birds?

Can birds turn their heads all the way in back of them?

Hearing and Making Sounds

Do birds have ears?

How do birds make their sounds?

We use most of the same materials and activities each time my class studies birds, yet these particular questions will never occur in just this way again. Each team of children and research helpers is unique, and will reveal its particular strengths and surprises as we learn together. Student-guided Internet research asks students to put to use what they are learning and wondering about, which continually leads them to new information, discoveries, and interconnections.

Chapter 3

Choosing a Topic for Long-term Student Research

Packing for a long trip far from home tends to unnerve me. I tend to worry that I'll forget something crucial or take something utterly useless that should have been left at home. When the packing is finally done and the bag is zipped, my worrying stops: Either I've picked the right things, or I'll survive somehow, mistakes and all.

Selecting a topic for student research can be seen as a similar task. Certain constraints and specific needs will guide your choice of what to study with your class. There's also the unknown which lies ahead of you. So you do your best to select what you hope will work during your year's travels with your class, and then learn whether your choices work well for this group or need some adjusting along the way. Last-minute items can, in fact, usually be borrowed, bought, or done without. We have similar opportunities to make needed changes along the way when we're using a long-term topic with children.

To continue the analogy, some people do better traveling as lightly and spontaneously as possible. They wear the clothes they're comfortable in, pack a couple of things in a backpack, and they're ready to go. This kind of adaptability is similar to teaching with a projects perspective rather than from a theme or topic. Let me explain the difference between these seemingly similar terms.

There's much current debate between using a *theme* approach for classroom study, or a project model. With a theme structure, the teacher chooses a topic and then guides student efforts, usually in specific, preordained directions toward a predestined goal. In contrast, *project-based* teachers observe, using notes or other records of student conversations and ideas, as well as speaking with students closely, all in order to learn what interests them. From this information, she then creates the structure, providing support and materials for those student interests to continue to develop over time and be acted upon in a variety of ways by the children themselves. For lively and opinionated debate on the distinction between theme and project-based teaching, you might want to subscribe to the Projects Listserv itself. The address for this listserv is given in the Appendix.

Your choice of topic will be guided by your interests, values, and personality, and those of your students, as well as your district's and state's curriculum requirements. I recommend that you try to blend a curricular goal with an interest of your students or your own, and then think of how you can use the Internet as a tool for personalized student research on this topic.

It's useful to keep the following questions in mind when considering in-depth, long-term classroom research projects:

- Is this a topic that my students and I can stay interested in for a fairly extended period of time?
- If not, is it preferable to have strong student interest with several shorter, perhaps related, projects?
- Is it a topic that will be appropriate for most of the students, considering their varied backgrounds, interests, maturity, and skill levels?
- Is the topic broad and open-ended enough to generate subtopics, to allow for individual student interests to develop, grow, and be pursued with enthusiasm?
- Is this topic likely to interest many e-mail correspondents or just a few? Topics that are more obscure will tend to give you fewer research helpers, while topics that are more common will naturally tend to attract a larger pool of potential correspondents. The topics we have used in our classroom so far—birds, insects, and

the forest—have proven rich enough for a year's study by my students. These are areas with enough experts and enthusiasts so that we were easily able to contact a good range of correspondents for help. When considering possibilities for long-term student research, you'll want to decide whether you and your class are drawn to mainstream ideas or to more obscure and unusual concepts and areas to focus on.

- Do you have at least a baseline idea of the information and experiences you'd like your students to receive while studying this topic? Do they? E-mail research, though powerful, isn't a magic wand. It can bring curriculum alive working in tandem with support, resources, and materials in your classroom.

To map out long-term research topics, I begin with a general sketch of what I think will happen during the year. I can refer back to this to help me plan for lessons on essential information, and I enjoy seeing where student curiosity and correspondents' replies lead us as well. I "web" these topics in a personal brainstorm session just as they occur to me, and keep this diagram in my lesson plan book to refer to when planning or getting resources for our class (see p. 26). I also do a similar web with the children early in the year about our topic, to see what interests them and what they feel they already know about the topic.

Why Use One Topic All Year?

Focusing on one major topic for an entire school year, while using e-mail helpers, has worked well for students, our correspondents, and me. By June, the children in years past would have already forgotten all but the most recent topics we had studied during the year. Being permitted to stay on a single large topic for so long allows children several luxuries they're seldom otherwise afforded in this speedy world of ours.

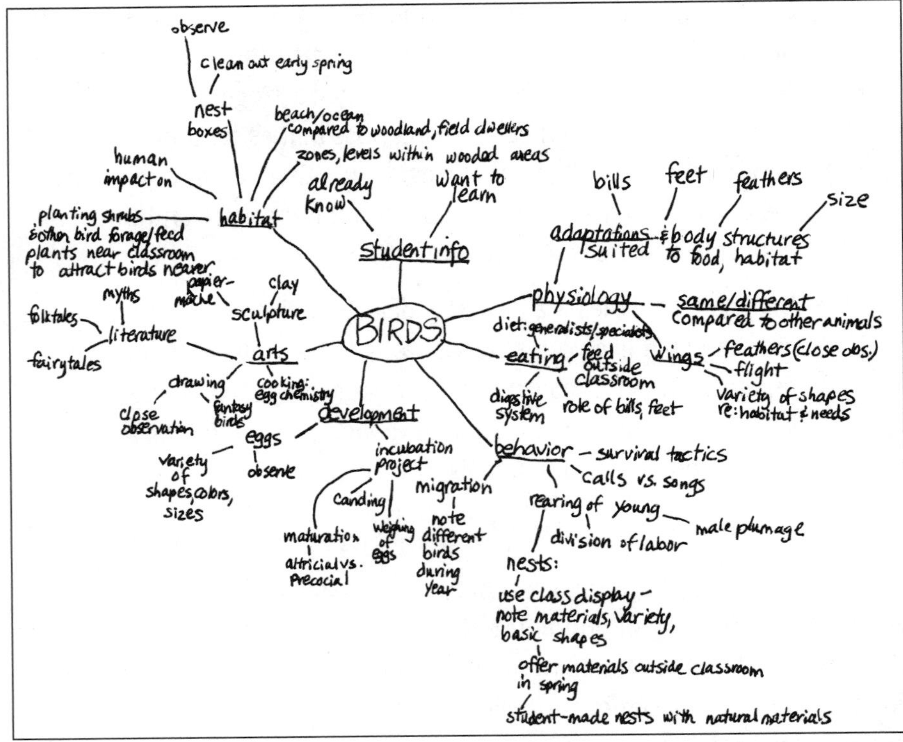

Webbing a topic is a useful tool to brainstorm possible areas to focus on. This can be done in two steps: an overview for planning by the teacher (shown here) and a whole-class preassessment to reveal existing student knowledge and areas of interest in the topic.

Some advantages I've seen with year-long study on a topic:

- The children are clear about what they are learning, because as a group they're sharing a deep and lasting awareness of something specific and fairly constant.
- There's enough time to allow the children to ask questions that are off-topic when something intrigues them. One year, we were studying birds, but the children were fascinated by a reference our Australian correspondent made about the noises he'd heard koalas making at night. They wrote to ask him to describe the sounds he'd heard, and we learned that koalas have a wide vocal range and are capable of growls and barks!

- Without a deadline for the project's end, we get to know our correspondents over time, as real people. One man wrote proudly, telling us of his baby daughter's first steps; graduate students described travels to study exotic birds in the Antarctic; and another student told us about his admission to a select high school and his out-of-school interests.
- We don't stop studying our topic at some arbitrary point in the year (until June, that is!). The normal model of sudden closure on a topic can sometimes give children the impression that "we're done with birds" (or whatever we've been studying together) and that it's now no longer a topic of interest.
- With a year's frame, I can allow the time necessary for learning to sift down and become owned by the learner, for ideas to dawn, for connections to be built among ideas, and for observations to support ideas to be made. And all this processing does take time.
- Student attention span for, and awareness of, the year's topic increase. Observing any group of my students from fall until spring, I can see their attention spans increase during hikes or other related activities. And I'm amazed when the group that couldn't watch quietly outdoors in September—the group that managed to scare away even the few birds brave enough to linger nearby—can now gaze happily and attentively in June while an osprey slowly dives three times into the bay directly below us. They truly know birds now, and they have shared an experience of engaged, long-term learning with each other and with our correspondents.

It might initially seem appealing to choose a topic for student Internet research about which you know little or nothing, and to rely heavily on your e-mail experts for the information that you lack. But my advice is to do exactly the opposite. Start with something you know, perhaps something you have already taught and, ideally, already love as a topic. Then let the e-mail experts share their knowledge, even when you may know the answer yourself. Here's why I suggest this so strongly:

First, you'll have a much better sense of the level of expertise of your potential correspondents if you have some prior knowledge of the subject. You can then judge for yourself from their writing just what they seem to know on your topic. Being familiar with the subject means that you will also be more skilled in determining whether or not potential correspondents are able to explain concepts and ideas clearly—and in an engaging manner—for your students.

Second, you won't be relying on this new experiment to make the topic worthwhile or rich enough to justify the time and effort you, your students, and your correspondents will be expending. You already know it's a strong topic, and you will be better able to provide hands-on lessons, readings, and special experiences both inside and outside the classroom. These initial and ongoing encounters with the topic all help to spark reflective thinking, which leads to lively and informed questions. Students will certainly be encouraged to question by having clear and enthusiastic correspondents, but their main springboard for wondering is still the stimulating climate we create in our classrooms.

Third, by working with a familiar topic, you will be leaving yourself the necessary luxury of some learning time to get even more familiar with the Internet. Using e-mail research with a known subject area is almost as though you are returning to a favorite camping spot, but with a much better tent. Remember to be patient with yourself—because it's new, that tent may well be tricky to set up the first few times.

Last, by using a topic that you are already comfortable with, you will have in mind some of the places your studies might take your students, as well as some likely side trips that may occur along the way. You can initiate a familiar topic more confidently, and you can better judge the appropriateness of students' questions for e-mail—or other forms of inquiry, such as reading, direct observation, and local experts. When possible, include other students in your school as informed experts on topics; it's a great lesson for the person posing the question and a very positive statement about peer expertise to both students!

Once we are launched on our topic, the children's questions often arise with a life of their own. I don't try to organize them or keep them on a particular topic, beyond the large one we are all exploring for the year. Some of our best exchanges have been off-topic, such as a rash of questions to our friends in Holland and Finland about the Northern Lights. These had nothing to do with our study of the forest, but everything to do with the return of a beloved librarian from her recent adventures in Alaska (where she had not been able to see this phenomenon for herself). We guessed that these people, our most northerly correspondents, might have some direct experience of the subject to share with us, and they told us fascinating things about aurora borealis.

Straying off-topic now and then—and letting questions on your topic arise spontaneously—permits us all to respond to the normally bouncy rhythms of engaged and curious minds. A mind working like this needs to leap around sometimes, with enough of a boundary to keep it manageable and anchored to a shared reality, yet open enough to permit true wondering to happen. The journey becomes far more interesting when we let ourselves wander occasionally, but still have a clear idea where our base is and where we will return again and again.

Some students are able to read their own e-mail replies to the class, especially if the print is enlarged for them.

Chapter 4 Getting Comfortable with the Internet

As teachers, we've all experienced the awkwardness of working with new materials or unfamiliar lessons. Our students can sense our discomfort. More importantly, we aren't able to enjoy the learning, our students, or ourselves as much as when we have had time to internalize what we are teaching and it comes from deep within us.

It's for this reason that I suggest you take the time—and it does take some time—to become familiar with the Internet before introducing it to your students as part of whatever curriculum you choose. I don't mean you must become an Internet expert before using it with your class! By its very nature the Internet is designed to constantly change and grow; being an expert on its every detail is impossible. But you will need to gain a basic familiarity with a few of its key information tools. Those I'll discuss in this chapter are websites, newsgroups, listservs, and e-mail. I think that you'll find the Internet is a user-friendly place to visit—a combination library, Yellow Pages, coffeehouse, university, post office, shopping mall, and entertainment center, all rolled into one. Although your first few ventures online may feel a little scary, with practice, you'll soon be using this technology just as naturally as you can now drive a car or use an answering machine.

Those of you who want more detailed information or need support to learn more about using the Internet will find that the bibliography at the end

of this book contains a list of resources that have been especially useful to my colleagues and me. It's beyond the scope of a book this size to serve as a complete handbook for using the Internet, but fortunately, there are many fine books and classes for beginners that can help get you started.

About Websites

Much like a book, a website contains information about a particular topic or available service. Most websites aren't primarily intended for personal exchanges, but to display information, products, or opinions. And most

Establishing and maintaining e-mail connections can be an opportunity for teacher growth and correspondence.

websites are not interactive. This simply means they aren't usually designed to change or reflect the opinions of people accessing them, as newsgroups and listservs are.

Websites often have "links," which are connections to other websites with related information. These links allow you to easily go to other websites, in order to read more on a topic that interests you. They help make navigating the Internet much easier; with a click of your mouse, they can automatically take you to other sites that are related to the topic you're learning about. For example, I was able to research an entire family vacation recently by just typing in the province of Canada we planned to visit. At the first website I reached, one about travel in British Columbia, I was shown many links to choose from. Some of these led me to information about the cities we wanted to visit, and other links guided me to discover an island I'd never heard of and which became our favorite part of the trip.

Every website has its own specific address, which usually, but not always, begins with "www" and is followed by a string of characters. For example, each of the following is a website address:

- www.mcn.org will take you to the website for Mendocino Community Network, an Internet Service Provider for my school district, as well as many businesses and services that advertise on it.
- quest.arc.nasa.gov will connect you with the NASA educational website, which has "gov" at the end of the URL, or address, because it's a government agency.
- web66.coled.umn.edu is a website listing many schools in the world that have their own websites.

If you don't have a specific address for a website, but want to see what's out there on your topic, many books are now available that list sites by categories (see Appendix). There are also lots of tools, called search engines, which enable your computer to help you explore and browse the World Wide Web. Search engines work like no other information tool we've ever had. When I use one, I have an image in my mind of an all-knowing genius who instantly knows what's listed in the card catalogue for every library in the world—plus everything else that's accessible electronically on our planet. A nice resource to call upon!

One of the interesting characteristics of search engines is that it's quite possible to uncover different resources by using different engines. Each imaginary genius has her own perspective and special interests, after all. Alta Vista is one common search engine (www.altavista.digital.com); other popular search engines today include Netscape Navigator (www.netscape.com), HotBot (www.hotbot.com), InfoSeek (www.infoseek.com), and Lycos (www.lycos.com). Discovering which one yields the best results for you is part of the fun of searching.

It takes patience and persistence to find hidden website treasures, but once you've found them, they're worth every bit of effort you've exerted. When you're conducting a search, remember that there's almost always a particular combination of words that will lead you somewhere worthwhile. Many strategies are suggested in books dealing with Internet use, which will make your search more efficient. For children, it can be like discovering a secret code or magic spell. When you get frustrated with a temporarily fruitless web search, remind yourself that however lengthy your search, it's far quicker than making dozens of phone calls, writing stacks of letters, or driving around the world looking for the same resources.

About Newsgroups

To me, newsgroups most resemble social groups that meet over time to share areas of common interest. We've all known students who spend almost every recess playing basketball, others who enjoy fantasy play in the sandbox, and still others who—literally—hang out on the bars. To become a newsgroup, these same children could discuss their feelings and suggest techniques about their favorite recess pastimes online, perhaps using a (mythical) newsgroup called "rec.monkeybars" or "rec.sandbox." There are currently over 26,000 newsgroups in existence. There probably will be quite a few more added by the time you read this, and there might well be one called "rec.monkeybars" among them!

A newsgroup, then, is a collection of people who are electronically connected and who share an interest they want to discuss with others. Instead of needing to ask if you can shoot a few hoops or help make the road in the sand, you need only search in your news reader program for groups that sound interesting to you. Once you've found a few to investigate, you can read messages posted by people who have written to that group.

The majority of posts on a newsgroup are either questions or answers, and they are usually brief. Sometimes there will be a "string," which is a series of separate comments made in response to one person's initial remark or question. In style, these generally tend to be less conversational than what you will read on a listserv. It seems to me that listservs are used more as a forum for extended inquiry or conversations, in which people get to know each other's biases and crotchets over time, while newsgroups serve people who want specific, pithy, short-term information or advice. However, some people who write to newsgroups are quite well informed about the topic and enjoy answering questions very much.

Children will often watch others playing, either waiting to find a good opening to ask if they can join, or simply for the entertainment offered by observing. The same behavior when applied to a newsgroup—to just read other people's posts (comments) without writing anything yourself—is called "lurking." It's perfectly acceptable online behavior, and a very good way to glean information as well. Once you have interacted with the group by posting your own comment or question, you will be seen as a full participant.

When you decide to participate in a newsgroup, you can immediately answer a comment someone else has written, or you can start a new topic (called a "thread") about anything related to that group's scope. Unlike a listserv, you do not need to subscribe, so you can write to the newsgroup as soon as you dare. Anyone reading the comment you've sent to that newsgroup can choose to ignore what you wrote, answer you directly (by using your e-mail address), or post her response to you for the entire group to read. Again, it's quite similar to conversing in a large group—sometimes a person will make an observation that catches everyone's interest, and other times, the remark goes by without further comment.

In daily life, you may meet someone, decide you want to get to know her better, and arrange to spend time together again. Similarly, it's quite possible to read comments written by someone on a newsgroup, and then begin to correspond directly with her by using her personal e-mail address, instead of continuing your conversation in front of the rest of the group.

When I'm looking for potential correspondents for my students on our focus topic, I've had excellent luck posting to a large group of people who are interested in our topic, and have also been very successful writing directly to individuals in those groups. I've enjoyed the sense of already slightly "knowing" someone before I request their help, after I've read several of their posts to a newsgroup. On the other hand, the initial request for volunteer experts that I once posted to a newsgroup was kindly forwarded by other participants in the group, and so my message reached people and places I could never have imagined finding on my own! This adventure began when I read a comment on the newsgroup "rec.birds," from someone whose address ended with "nl." I (correctly) guessed that the abbreviation meant "Netherlands." Because I had wanted to try extending our correspondence beyond the United States for the first time, I wrote to him and asked for help with our research project. He was unable to help us, yet kindly forwarded my request to a European bird newsgroup, where it was posted for me by the highly regarded moderator himself. This gracious and unexpected publicity brought us an entirely new and varied group of delightful experts from all over Europe.

A word of friendly caution: Newsgroups are so very public that your comments can be disseminated worldwide in a matter of seconds. Your thoughts are no longer private once you send them out onto a newsgroup or a listserv, nor is your e-mail address. It's wise to proceed with caution and discretion whenever you consider posting to a group.

Some groups are formed capriciously or too optimistically. These newsgroups will reveal no postings at all when you try to select them, because no one has chosen to write to them. Other newsgroups are incredibly busy places, where a constant stream of commentary and ideas flows among the participants. As a starting place, you might want to visit these newsgroups, lurk a bit, and see which appeal to you:

k12.chat.teacher	k12.music
k12.ed.art	k12.science
k12.ed.comp.literacy	k12.lang.art
k12.math	k12.news

Quantity does not always mean quality in a newsgroup, however, and sometimes newsgroups that look very active and show a high number of postings (messages) will turn out to have high rates of off-topic or marginally useful comments, or advertisers sneaking in and trying to sell their products online.

You might want to practice your newsgroup skills by lurking around a group that shares an interest or a hobby with you. Some possible groups to investigate are rec.birds, rec.music, rec.antiques, rec.books, misc.fitness.walking, and rec.dancing. When you've found a group that sounds worthwhile, don't feel obligated to participate immediately! I've found lurking to be much like politely joining any other conversation that's already in progress. Wait to get a sense of the history, tone, and content of the conversation before making your own comments; you can learn a great deal about the topic and the participants, and you can also save yourself lots of potential embarrassment by not speaking too soon.

Occasionally, people online can be very impatient with newcomers, with those they feel are uninformed, or with someone they think isn't using proper online procedures or etiquette. Sending an extremely unkind or severely critical message is called "flaming," and it's usually an unforgettable lesson in caution for the person who gets flamed. Flaming isn't acceptable online behavior, but it happens to the best of us. I've learned to always assess the territory before jumping into online discussions with my own opinions, and I read my own messages several times before I post them. I want to be sure the meaning is clear, the message is worth sending, and the tone is as friendly as possible when I post something for the world to read.

Here's a further argument in support of watchful waiting: We are often better at absorbing unfamiliar information when we're not trying to participate at the same time. You may feel like you're listening in on a telephone conversation, but there's an important difference between regular eavesdropping and lurking on a newsgroup. The in-person conversations are intended to be private, while the newsgroup, by definition and expectation, is clearly public.

You will probably want to thoroughly check several possible groups while you're considering a topic for in-depth student inquiry. Sometimes you will find collaborators in surprising places on the Internet. Be creative, and look for a variety of newsgroups that might interest the kind of person you would like your students to be able to correspond with.

About Listservs

Imagine innocently requesting "More Information" on an advertisement and mailing it in. Months later, you realize your mailbox is bursting with catalogues and other advertisements you don't remember asking for: Your name must have been sold to other mailing lists. In a way, subscribing to a listserv resembles this avalanche of mail, because once you have subscribed to a listserv, you will automatically be sent (as e-mail) every correspondence that the group receives. The difference is that the messages you are sent will be from the same group, the listserv you subscribed to. The good news and the bad news are the same: You can find yourself getting huge amounts of mail this way. If you have plenty of time and the listserv discussions are interesting to you, this can be good. If not, you may find yourself soon growing weary of all the mail you are being sent by a listserv.

You can participate in a listserv only if you subscribe to it. It's a closed system, but it's not very exclusive in most cases. Some groups are moderated carefully, which means there is a list manager who reads all the mail, and sometimes even decides who can join the listserv. There are usually guidelines beyond simple common sense for participating in these listservs, and if you break the group's rules of conduct, you can be censured or even dropped from the list. Some groups limit the number of postings permitted by an individual within a given time, in order to allow broader participation from the group. This is especially helpful if a group has a very large membership and many of the same people tend to post over and over again. Another advantage of moderated lists is that someone is in charge and can step in if a discussion gets unfriendly, off-topic for that group, or unproductive.

If you do choose to subscribe to a listserv, read the subscriber information you are sent *very carefully*. Be very sure to save the instructions you're sent on how to unsubscribe! I have a folder in my e-mail files which

I've labeled simply "unsubscribe," and it contains the exact words and addresses I will need if I choose to stop receiving mail from any listserv I have subscribed to. I file the information about how to unsubscribe from each listserv as soon as I receive it. These instructions and addresses are specific to each group, and I strongly suggest you create a special place on your computer to save this information, and choose a file name for that information which will be easy for you to remember.

Without this information, you may become desperate enough about dropping from a listserv to commit an Internet *faux pas*. Though many people do so, it's considered very bad "netiquette" to post to an entire group when you decide to unsubscribe or want information on how to do this because you didn't save the instructions you were sent when you first subscribed. When you post "unsubscribe" to the whole group, you often don't get the information you want, and it annoys all those particpants who expect interesting items—not requests to unsubscribe—to be e-mailed to them from the listserv. Imagine if you or another guest loudly announce that you're bored and want to leave a party, rather than quietly departing and letting the other guests continue to enjoy themselves without being so rudely interrupted. Announcing your wish to "unsubscribe" to the reading public, rather than to the list manager who handles these requests, is the same kind of intrusion.

About E-mail

Of all the resources on the Internet, e-mail is probably most like one we already use daily: postal mail. Each person has her own address and can be contacted directly, instead of writing to a newsgroup or posting on a listserv. To receive e-mail, you need only give your address to another person and check occasionally—or more often, if you're like me—to see if you have new messages to read and answer. And as my father taught me when I was little, if you want to get mail, you need to send mail!

Despite its similarity to postal mail, there are some unique conventions that most people observe when sending e-mail. One example is that writers rarely begin e-mail messages with the formal "Dear . . ." salutation, but instead tend to use more casual variations for a greeting. Some people jump right into the message itself, with no salutation; others begin with the addressee's name or "Hi." Sentences may be shorter than in a paper letter. There are often no paragraph indentations; instead, a blank line is used between two unrelated ideas or chunks of writing.

It's important to make your e-mail communication very clear to the reader, and this can be a challenge. E-mail letters are consistently formed in a generic font, with no handwriting and obviously no facial or voice cues to help us gauge the writer's personality or mood. People who use listservs in particular can become quite upset with another writer when messages are written so tersely or quickly that their meaning isn't made clear enough. Paying attention to the tone of your writing when you use this form of communication is a real art; your efforts will reward you with communications with others that are more productive as well as having fewer electronic misunderstandings. To lighten the mood or show feeling, some writers include occasional "smileys" in their messages. These punctuation faces, when read sideways, can help the reader interpret sentences meant to show irony ; -) —perhaps even flirting!—or happiness : -) or other feelings not conveyed by plain type. One boy in my class even invented a bird smiley : ^ for a special e-mail he was sending to one of our correspondents.

Using all uppercase letters in any communication makes it hard for most readers to easily read what's written, since the letters are all the same size—and in e-mail, it's interpreted as shouting! However, some common phrases are capitalized and abbreviated: Two you may see often on postings to newsgroups are IMHO, which stands for "In My Humble Opinion," and BTW, which means "By The Way."

E-mail was originally intended to be quick and efficient, a businesslike means of communicating electronically. It can indeed be used like a telegram, with only the basics included. However, in the hands of some writers—for example, my high school English teacher, who sends me lavish descriptions of his travels—it can become just as eloquent and detailed as any paper letter. And there's the added advantage that it's instantly available to the reader as soon as it has been sent. It's tempting to feel you have to respond fast when using such a quick medium; I usually try to reread any letter several times before I send it. This allows me to edit, revise, and correct until the letter says precisely what I want it to say, and helps me refine phrases to limit misunderstandings and clarify meaning.

After you have some familiarity with websites, newsgroups, e-mail, and perhaps listservs, you can begin to think of them in terms of your students and the project ahead. Make a list of possible correspondents for your students or yourself, based on your impressions and observations over time. It's been helpful for me to keep an Internet notebook. I use it to write each person's e-mail address and a brief note about where on the Internet we encountered each other (which newsgroup, listserv, etc.). Sometimes, I also use the notebook to write an address and comments about a listserv, website, or newsgroup that I am interested in learning more about. This information can help me decide later whether or not to subscribe, and to trace where I first found out about it.

You're likely to discover different strengths and weaknesses in all of these Internet resources, and to find them more or less appropriate for different uses. It's a little like creating a balanced diet: If you sample deliberately from them all, you can provide for a tremendous variety of needs and tastes while you continue to learn about and enjoy using the Internet.

Chapter 5

Getting Started with E-pals and Practicing Good Netiquette

Asked about his minister to Spain, Thomas Jefferson is said to have replied, "I haven't heard from him in two years. If I don't hear from him next year, I will write him a letter." At that time, the exchange of letters required substantially more than the click of a mouse. A correspondent not only needed to be literate (or to engage the services of someone else who was), but also be able to find a way to convey the letter to the recipient (good connections with horse riders and people traveling by boat to Europe were quite helpful), and, finally, one apparently needed to be very patient!

Were he alive now, I doubt that Jefferson would check his e-mail several times a day as I, and many of my favorite e-mail correspondents, do. Most of us now, if we write them at all, tend to take the getting and sending of letters for granted. The e-mail project in our class has been able to restore to correspondence some of the pleasure and the art it once possessed.

For long-term e-mail research to work well, you'll need to find people who share your enthusiasm for writing about mutual interests, whether these topics are your students' or your own. When you compose your request for correspondents, be pleasant as well as clear about your goals and expectations. Warm and precise communication from the start helps everyone feel comfortable and understand their role in your project. Here is a sample letter, similar to what I posted to newsgroups when asking for volunteers to help in our very first e-mail research project:

> We are a class of 1st and 2nd graders in Northern California. We will be spending this school year studying ____ and are looking for people all over the U.S., possibly beyond, who are willing and able to be patient and informed correspondents on our topic. We are interested in getting to know our helpers during the school year, thinking about our topic in some depth, and will be sending out student's questions as they occur during our studies. Thanks for any help!

Once you have located a few likely newsgroups or listservs, you can use them to post a message similar to the one above. You can choose to send your request to an entire group, or just to the individuals whose writing has especially interested you. If you post to a group, this will give your request greater exposure to more possible helpers; however, if you write directly to the people whose skills seem to fit your project, you can maintain more privacy and control over who is writing to you.

How to Choose?

When I begin an Internet quest to find e-mail research partners who might be interested in writing to our class, here's what I look for:

- What is the general tone of the group or writer? Do participants treat each other kindly, sharing information and opinions pleasantly and enthusiastically?
- Which people seem to truly enjoy answering others' questions, showing interest and patience, as well as knowledge of the topic?
- Who seems to have special areas of expertise that apply well to the topic?
- Who writes warmly and directly to the person whose question they are answering?
- Whose answers do I find myself enjoying and thinking about?

As you've read comments and messages on the Internet, you may have already begun to keep a list of likely correspondents for yourself or your students. A notebook is a good way to help you keep track of these people as individuals. Without the usual embodied context to rely on, correspondents on the Internet can "look" the same, and it's easy to get confused about who's who in the beginning. This is especially true if you are writing to quite a few people who are new to you. You can use this notebook to write the location on the Internet where you encountered each person, what you liked about their messages, what they seem to be interested in, where they live, and how often they appear to have time to write. These are all valuable clues to a person's suitability as a classroom correspondent.

Before you invite these people into the class to join your project, it's wise to get to know them a bit better via e-mail. Exchanging even a few notes, adult to adult, before students begin sending out their own questions, will give you a much clearer sense of these potential volunteers and their skills as helpers for your students. I ask each person I've selected to send us a brief personal background sketch. These miniature autobiographies provide wonderful introductions when children first learn about the people they will be writing to all year. These personal stories can give us many fascinating insights about our helpers. They help start our e-mail relationships in a direct and personal way, and they help make these year-long connections strong and vivid for young children. Here's a selection from the background letter sent to us by a Finnish graduate student:

> . . . It was a greatest experience to grow up that little starving pityful chick into a majestic bird. As we were with my friend having our Army duty in an isolated fortress island in Gulf of Finland, there's a ravens family living in the island. They had about four or five chicks, but because raven is a predator, it often happens that when they have many chicks, the youngest one is so much smaller than the bigger ones that it is the weakest (and) can't get food enough, leaves starving and finally is eaten by its brothers and sisters. That's a cruel nature law—the youngest

> one is an allowance chick which is laid to grow up if the older chicks for some reason die or if the food situation is so good that all the chicks can be grown. We noticed the situation and decided to commit a crime and interfere in nature's laws. We took away the youngest one. Then it was already starving, blind and featherless, at the same time as the others were almost ready to fly. . . . In three months the hopeless creature which we never really believed to survive, grew up into a huge black bird, extremely intelligent and "human," with its certain specific habits. . . . Once it started to steal socks from the house of my friend and took them to the roof. When this action was noticed, it was strictly told, that's not acceptable. It looked sad, walked away, quiet, and after a while we noticed it is carrying the socks BACK from the roof, one by one! . . . It is yes understandable that that kind of animal is not suitable to be a pet."

The letter continues, explaining this bird's eventual placement with another raven, living in the countryside while still young enough to perhaps choose to live wild, as the writer hoped. My students listen intently, looking concerned as they imagine the raven chick's rescue from certain death, and later laugh with relief when they hear the sock-stealing episode.

As you can see, the writer has shared some basic realities and laws of nature, as well as the effects and ethics of interfering with those—along with his great sense of humor. Years later, he remains a popular correspondent with our class, because of his unique experiences with birds and his warmth.

How Much Is Enough?

Now that you've considered who is likely to be a good correspondent for your class, and perhaps have chosen a few people to help your project, there are two more major questions to consider: How many correspondents will your class need for an effective and exciting e-mail research project? And, how do you maintain interest and connection with these valuable resource people over the course of a school year? These questions, when answered well, will keep an e-mail project rolling smoothly rather than allow it to falter or die prematurely.

The ideal number of correspondents? Simply put, you'll want enough people to provide students with variety and dependability in their answers, yet few enough to allow you to keep track of them well. A group of between five and seven people seems to work well for us. We once worked with fifteen, located all over the world. It was almost an embarrassment of riches, though we certainly got amazing and varied responses that year.

A group of five to seven correspondents gives you—as well as them—necessary flexibility. Some helpers may not answer regularly or promptly; others might not answer e-mail after having expressed their interest in the project. Your helpers will have family or social obligations, vacations, and responsibilities—sometimes with deadlines—at work or school. Allow for the possibility that someone on your list might turn out to be less than an ideal match for your particular group or topic. Working with between five and seven people also gives your students a manageable variety of perspectives, locales, and areas of special expertise among the people you choose to write.

How much do they need to know? Will you want to have research helpers who have very specific areas of expertise, or people who are very enthusiastic but perhaps not experts on the subject? Each of these has its advantages and drawbacks. A combination of several approaches and a variety of correspondents provide the richest mix for children to choose among. Experts who know only their own subject, however deeply, may not be able to clearly share their knowledge and excitement about the subject with young children. Novice enthusiasts may not provide much new information for your students, but they can give your students a terrific model of adults learning, with delight, alongside children. We've found both perspectives very useful in our work, and in our experience, quite a few of our correspondents manage to combine their far-ranging knowledge with contagious enthusiasm about the subject and a gift for explaining things well to the children.

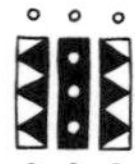

Maintaining the Flow

Once you've begun direct communication with people interested in helping your students, you'll want to notice how quickly they're able to respond to questions, and how thorough their replies are. Immediacy, especially with young children, is a strong factor in the success of an e-mail project. Many questions have a limited shelf life; left unanswered for too long, they may die a quiet death, and this neglect can discourage further inquiry by students.

I try to answer people immediately when they express an interest in helping with our projects. I do this for two reasons: I want to set a tone of polite gratitude, which I indeed feel, and I want to let them know I'm thinking of their convenience as well as the contribution they will be making to our class during the year. Most people who write to my students make a tremendous gift to us of their time, effort, and knowledge. It's very important

Students may send joint questions, or listen in on another's letter while waiting their turn at the computer.

to me that they know how deeply the children and I appreciate their generosity and expertise.

I also tell volunteers that we won't begin corresponding as soon as school starts. We need to set up a class routine first, settle in, and figure out how we all fit together before introducing more people into our mix for the year. We need to set the stage effectively with the children, both for the project's content and for the people we'll be learning about and from. The children need time and opportunities to become clear about what they already know about the topic and what they would like to investigate.

I've said that I try to write to each person several times on my own before school begins. By doing this, I can establish a personal base with them and get a clearer idea about how often they check—and how quickly they usually answer—their e-mail. I can find out how long and how detailed their replies generally are. I want to maintain contact with, and the interest of, our helpers, not leave them to wonder if we've forgotten them or don't appreciate their offer to assist us. Because we may not start sending e-mail till October or later, my occasional letters to our helpers during that time are intended to reassure them that we are sincere and grateful.

When you reply to volunteers interested in helping your class, it's helpful to restate, briefly but clearly, your goals for the project. It's important that both the project and our methods are well understood by the people working with us. Knowing what to expect lets them participate with us more comfortably and appropriately. A friend of mine calls this "checking for understanding," and it works wonders for all forms of communication. I let our helpers know that the questions will come in no particular order or rhythm, directly from the students' experiences and thinking. Then our correspondents know to expect the unexpected, and that our primary goal for them is to help support and inform inquiry by these young children.

You may want to base your research on student interest, rather than planning for a topic before school begins. Be sure to budget the time you'll need once school starts, to permit you to gather a group of correspondents and materials for any project on a student-generated topic. For any new area of focus, my preparation will include hours of reading comments on related newsgroups and listservs, then writing to individuals. This is how I assemble our working list of the people who will help us.

I usually like to return to school in the fall with a list of e-mail helpers for the coming year. This gives me the assurance that our research assistants are already in place, waiting to hear from the children once school begins. Planning ahead gives me the summer to collect books and other materials useful to the project we will be working on during the year. Yet, many teachers find working directly from student interest—rather than from teacher plans—has an excitement and an authenticity worth the ongoing search for materials and resources which this approach requires.

Keeping the Relationships Working Well

I always screen the children's e-mail questions before we send them. I do this for two reasons: to be considerate of our helpers, and to help develop good research and thinking skills in the children. I won't let my students send e-mail questions that can be answered more appropriately by other means. A student who wonders what color a Western Gull's legs are is directed to the field guides in our science center, or is asked to look on top of the light pole outside of our classroom—where one of these scavengers is usually perched. In this situation, the bird itself might answer the child's question most effectively!

I let both the children and our potential correspondents know about our rule for sending only questions that are suited to e-mail inquiry. This helps us to not trivialize our e-mail relationships and encourages the children to rely on themselves. They learn to choose from a range of resources when they are wondering about something on our topic. I ask that my students—as much as possible—interact with our correspondents as respectful colleagues. Our helpers can in turn trust us to send them worthwhile, appropriate questions that come from sincere interest on the children's part.

Though the questions come from the children, I try to personally answer any letters the class receives during weekends, and especially those that arrive over school vacations. The children will later send their own response and thanks, but until they are able to do this, I want the writer to know that her message arrived and was appreciated. Of course, this isn't absolutely necessary in order to make the project work—I just happen to love writing to people. I have also found that I can learn much more about some of our correspondents if I sometimes write to them, in addition to the letters that are sent by the children.

At the first chance, I ask a child who has recently received an e-mail reply to sit with me at the computer. Together, we write a thank-you for the response they received, along with any further thoughts or questions the student may have. Good manners create good connections among people; that is one of the primary lessons in our e-mail research partnerships.

I will occasionally encourage a child to send the same question to more than one person, so she can receive a range of answers and perspectives to consider. And occasionally, a correspondent simply can't answer a particular question for us; students enjoy being able to then teach an adult what we have learned from another e-mail helper who was asked the same question.

As with any other relationship, writing to e-mail research assistants takes practice, care, and time to unfold and become rewarding. It grows stronger and more engaging when we use deliberate communication, clear responses, and positive comments. Children who use this dynamic form of inquiry are learning these real-world lessons, along with the information they request in their own letters.

Chapter 6

Introducing the Concept—and the Correspondents—to Students

It's easy for me to remember to introduce people to each other—as long as they've already met! I often tend to forget this crucial formality when I'm with two people who haven't met before and actually need an introduction. As a teacher, I'm constantly reminded that introductions and beginnings can powerfully influence the quality of learning in my classroom. This is why, before I begin talking with my students about our e-mail research project, I prepare carefully, using just a few important materials to help make these first impressions of our research helpers memorable for the children.

When I ask the children to gather at the rug to first "meet" our e-mail correspondents, I have a stack of very small cards on which I've written each research person's name and a few words to identify their area of interest or expertise. I also have two laminated maps—a large one of the United States and an even larger world map—as well as a roll of clear tape and our almost-empty e-mail binder. When we begin, the only letters in this binder are the autobiographical sketches I've requested and received from each of our e-mail helpers. I feel a familiar delight, knowing that this empty binder is about to change forever as we settle down at the rug together.

I tell the children first how lucky they are: There are people all over the United States—or the world, depending on our scope this time—who are experts on our topic for the year. I explain that although these people all go

to school or to work, although they have friends and family to keep them busy, they are eager to help answer the questions we will raise this year about our topic. I tell the children that we won't meet these people in real life—at least not usually—but that we will get to know them by writing to them on our computer, which easily allows us to send our questions and receive their answers all year long.

Because I want the children to see each person who writes to us as an individual, it's very important that we talk about each of them in detail and somehow give them a physical presence in our room. One correspondent e-mailed a digitized photo of herself and two colleagues, which is taped on the cabinet above our computer! I've found that the large maps we use to locate our e-mail friends in the world are an effective method to help children visualize our correspondents in a more concrete way than e-mail permits. When we refer to the maps and talk about our helpers around the world, we also develop strong geography skills in a context that has meaning for young children.

Improved geography skills and interest are another benefit of e-mail research.

My students and I talk about how they're going to come up with their own questions on our topic. I tell the children that they can choose whom to write to, any time they have a question for one of our experts. I want them to know that every person on our maps has slightly different information to share with us and that there are aspects of our subject that interest each of them. Because our correspondents have already written a bit about themselves for us, I've used this information to distill a few key words onto the cards we'll soon tape to the maps. Below each person's name, I've noted "bird habitat consultant" or "graduate student, farm bird/road-building ecology" or "university biology professor." We talk about what these long words mean and what kinds of jobs these people are doing. I include all this information so we can better remember each of the people we write to, and to help the children make the best possible choice when selecting which person to send their question. Here is another excerpt:

> I started to get seriously interested in wildlife when I was in the third grade. We did a big section in our science class all about ecology. I was fascinated by food webs from the very beginning, everything is connected to everything else. To me, it just makes an absolutely beautiful sort of sense, how nature works together and doesn't waste anything. I was especially fascinated by the 'circle of life'—how when things die, decomposers (bacteria, funguses, etc.) break them back down into nutrients that plants need to grow. It was also about the third grade that I began to get into the political side of the environment. I read a lot of wildlife magazines, and learned about how some organizations were working to get laws passed to help protect wildlife. I even joined some [of] these organizations. I read everything I could about wildlife (I was a real bookworm). I also read a lot of other stuff which (I didn't know it then) turned out to be very important for my development. I like mysteries and science fiction a lot. Both are about figuring things out, which is what science is about too.

> A lot of time passed, and I got interested in other things, but two of my favorites were always science and politics. Science helps us know what the world is really like, and politics is about having the power to change it. . . .

We read each of the stories our helpers have written for us, and as we finish hearing each one, students help attach the corresponding label to one of the maps. As we do this, we talk about the countries, states, and cities we recognize. Children make connections to places their families are from or have talked about or visited, as well as locations we've sung or read about. This is one of the most important parts of our project: We will get to learn *about* as well as *from* the people with whom we correspond. The children will discover shared interests with people all over the world, although their lives may be very different. This is a crucial piece of knowledge as we approach the end of the century. It embodies the miracle of this new form of communication: Using the Internet, we can discover quickly and easily the heartening truth that there are more similarities than differences between people, more points of connection than dissension among us all.

My young students are warmly accepted by our helpers as fellow scientists in the larger world. To have this demonstrated daily is a wonderful experience at any age. The fact that it's accomplished electronically, and sometimes in the space of minutes, makes it all the more exciting and useful to our class. So we talk next about how we will thank these generous people every time we've enjoyed and learned from an answer we've received from them. I explain that only when we write back to our e-mail helpers will they know we got their letters and what we learned from them. We want these people to stay interested in helping us, and the children begin to see that they can influence the success of the project with their own writing.

I tell the children that sometimes an answer they get might make them think of a new question, or it may not teach them all they wanted to know. My continuing second-grade students remember this, and can talk with the new first-graders about how it works. They have learned that we can choose to write back to someone again, asking for further clarification, or we might want to send the same question to more than one person. The following chapter offers more thoughts on the importance of helping children think clearly about their questions and evaluate the answers they receive. It also suggests a variety of strategies that will help keep an e-mail research project alive and well.

It's too much to include during the introductions session, so I try in a later meeting at the rug to give my students a simplified explanation of how e-mail on the Internet works. I tell the children that the words we type on our classroom computer are put into code inside our computer, and they are then sent through more wires to the high school in town (which is where our Internet service provider is). Next, the code is sent through more wires very quickly to another powerful computer, located near the person they're writing to. That computer sends our message to the person's own computer, kind of like a relay race, and there the student's original message finally gets changed back to the words we typed in our computer. After our correspondent checks her mail, she reads it when she has time, and answers it after she's thought about the question (and perhaps done some research on it as well). This process is definitely more abstract than the way our town's post office functions, but I want the children to have at least a very basic idea about what happens between our sending a question and receiving a reply. As I wrote this passage, I decided to ask my students to act out the roles in this scenario; passing a written message among several children, positioned around our classroom, may help them symbolically "see" the many connections that occur each time we send and receive e-mail. And I will also remind myself that, even after several years of constant practice with e-mail, it's still quite magic to me—wires and all.

Chapter 7

Strategies to Help Internet Work Run Smoothly

You may have a classroom like mine—one that any detective or archaeologist would appreciate for its layers of clues and artifacts. Perhaps, like me, you're also trying to pare down and tidy up the stuff in your life. This chapter will offer a variety of ideas to help you and your students learn to keep track of—and enjoy—the mail that your project will generate. Clutter prevention is fairly universal, whether it concerns real paper or e-mail: Take care of things as they arise (or as soon as possible), then discard or file them systematically for later use. Fortunately, this kind of "virtual housekeeping" is less work and much easier to organize than the tangible clutter some of us are so expert at accumulating.

Once your class begins corresponding with volunteer researchers, new classroom jobs and responsibilities that never before existed may occur to you and your students. Sharing responsibility for the upkeep with students will teach them valuable skills, as well as help everyone involved get the most benefit possible from the mail you send and receive. Here are some ways we manage our e-mail, to keep it both fluid and productive.

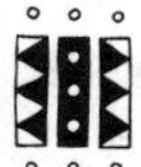

The Computer Expert

If you have a computer in your classroom or accessible at your school, you might want to consider adding "Computer Expert" to your list of student

jobs. We brainstorm jobs each fall after we've spent a week or two in school and write them on a long chart. Computer Expert is usually a favorite job and is enjoyed by my students. It carries lots of privileges, including frequent trips to the office to retrieve our new mail once it is printed.

Training a student to check for new e-mail on the class or school computer can be easier than teaching an adult to do the same job. Remember that the students who perform this task are being given the power to read all e-mail on the machine, as well as to delete anything (whether by accident or intent). If you're comfortable delegating this much power to a student, you'll naturally want to start with children you trust and who enjoy being reliable.

Here's what the Computer Experts in our class do:

- Turn on the computer each morning.
- Open and check our e-mail.
- Read the names of people on the screen. Those who can't read the names spell them to me. We decide if a message is likely to be about their bird research or is personal e-mail for me, because both arrive on our classroom computer. The children quickly learn to recognize the names of most of our e-mail correspondents, and they're especially skilled at identifying names of people to whom they've sent their own questions.
- When a new message is a reply to a student question, the Computer Expert opens it, reads it with me, and usually prints two copies of it.
- The Expert gets to walk down to the office where our printer is located and retrieve those printed copies of e-mail for us.
- One copy of the new message is delivered to the child to whom it was directed, and the other is given to me. I'll share it with the class, then file it in our class binder where we store all the e-mail responses we get during the year.
- I read the messages with the class during our group times, so the message waits on my lesson plan book till the next chance to share it.

- Whenever our computer beeps during the day, signaling new mail, the Computer Expert hurries to the monitor to see what we've just received. She follows the retrieval steps in this list.

Children take home their own e-mail letters, which is a good way of letting the parents see firsthand the special quality of the correspondence between our experts and their child. I also like the children to have their own copy of the letter because it's a tangible acknowledgment of the power of their own thinking and wondering.

Storing the Messages

When I first began the project, I arranged the binder for our e-mail chronologically, putting the most recent messages at the front of the binder. We found that this made it difficult and time-consuming to refer back to earlier messages. Together, the students and I decided to try filing our messages by categories. We brainstormed all the topics we had sent e-mail about, and I made index dividers for each. Then, whenever new mail was read, the children told me which section of the binder that particular letter should be placed in. More "thinking about thinking" occurred, and the children themselves had a much clearer idea where to look when we wanted to cross-reference something or remember a reply we'd received.

Storing these messages from correspondents on your computer is even easier, yet very useful as well for later reference. Simply create a folder in your "Transfer" menu option, name it something straightforward and memorable (like "Bird E-mail 1997–98"), and each time mail has been read and answered by your students, the letter can be easily filed in that folder. If you don't do this periodically, you will find your e-mail "in" box soon looks like those wooden trays in cartoons of office desks: piled high and discouraging to sort through.

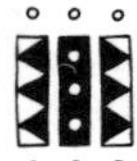

Keeping Track of the Unsent Questions

While the job of checking for new mail belongs to one or two children a week, the job of coming up with questions belongs to the entire class all year long. My stimulating tasks are to invite those questions, to read stories, to provide memorable experiences. I also am learning to listen more attentively to children's conversations, so that I can better support student thinking and mental meandering. I have a new role, keeping the interaction between my students and our e-mail helpers working smoothly for us all.

It's crucial to have a system to help you remember the questions your students come up with, until you have time to write and send them. We've tried a variety of ways to keep track of the childrens' questions as they occur; some have worked some of the time, some have not seemed too helpful, and

"I Am Wondering" sheets can help guide student questions to the most appropriate resources for answers.

others truly support the project and put the children in charge of their own thinking. Because keeping track of the questions is the first step in honoring children's wondering, it's essential that you find a method that works well for you and your students. I hope the ideas that follow will help, or will perhaps suggest other approaches that best suit you and your class.

Write down questions as soon as they are asked. Use large chart paper so you have a reminder on the wall, or write on the blackboard, or in a notebook stored near your meeting circle, which can be carried over to the computer when it's time to send messages. Older students can write their own questions to send later.

Our newest—and still experimental—approach comes from the work of Helen DePree. Using our "I Am Wondering" form gives the student a framework for remembering and proceeding with the research about their own questions (see examples on pages 60 and 61).

This record also can make wondering, and following through on those ideas, a more normal part of life in your classroom. Children are reminded directly on the form itself that there are always several approaches and resources available to help pursue an answer to most questions. Computer research is probably the most glamorous of those resources, but it's up to us to think carefully in each case about which approach really suits the particular question at hand. This working document helps students articulate their initial questions, then guides them to choose resources to answer those questions, and, finally, completes the circle by encouraging them to assess their learning and share information with others.

Discussion and reflection over time are also excellent ways for children to discover the different options available to them as students and wonderers. They can see what worked for another child, observe others using various resource materials, and learn what works best for them in a given situation.

Students learn that there will be times when a book, CD-ROM, direct observation or experimentation, or a phone call to a local expert will be the most useful and reasonable approach. There will be other times when e-mail resource people are the best choice possible. We've often found that a combination of resources works best.

Name Hannah

Date April 17, 1997

I Am Wondering

My question is: Is there an umbilillckl cord in birds like humans?

I think that maybe Yes, to get food.

I will find out by: reading ☑ asking people ☑

sending email ☑ observing ☐ experimenting ☐

A completed set of "I Am Wondering" pages track students' questions and encourage sharing of what was learned.

What helped me the most was: Email. and my mom

What I learned was: They have a little string that give the baby food inside the egg! It is absorbed through a string! From the yolk!

"I Am Wondering" pages continued

Creating and Sending the E-mail Question

Once the children have decided that e-mail might be a helpful route to the answer they're seeking, I ask them to tell me what their basic question is, or to read it from their "I Am Wondering" sheet. We then sit at the computer to begin their letter.

At this point, we follow some fairly ritualized steps. These seem to make the process work more successfully, and they remind the children what a privilege it is to be able to send questions to these friendly strangers and look forward to solid, interesting replies as we do.

- We use conventional spelling for any student work that leaves the classroom. Temporary, or invented, spelling is an important stage for young children in their growth as writers, but we want our e-mail requests to be easily comprehended and accessible to all our correspondents, especially those who live outside the United States and are using English as a second language.
- I do the typing for the children. Teachers know only too well how little time there is in each day to give each child. Because my students are not yet skilled keyboard users, I choose to focus on getting their questions out to our correspondents rather than on letting each child type their own letters.
- We do, however, proofread together the message I've typed with the child. We make sure the question is as clear as possible and that the grammar and spelling are correct. Students see the real value and need to proofread, especially when working with a typist as inaccurate as I am.
- We talk about which of our correspondents might be the most informed about—or interested in—that particular child's question. We might get up and go look at one of our two maps to remind ourselves where our helpers live and what they're especially interested in. Or we might look through the e-mail binder to refresh our memories about who's most informed on the topic. Sometimes we will look back at previous letters, just to be sure

that we're not repeating a question that's already been answered. And other times, a child may not have a new question, but instead wants to build on a previous answer, either to get more information or to state his opinion or share the class reaction to that letter. Looking back over the letters in the binder helps this child clarify what he is writing about.

- Now we are ready to type in the address of the person this student has chosen to receive her question. I might remind the child where that person lives, and we can sometimes notice geographic clues in the address itself. (See Appendix for a list of international two-letter country codes in e-mail addresses.) Right next to our computer is a complete list of every correspondent and their e-mail address. This makes typing addresses quick and easy. I have children either read the address to me as I type it, or I occasionally ask the child to type the address herself. We carefully check any address for errors before sending the message.
- I ask the students what they think we should type in the area as their "Subject." This step helps the children focus again on what their question is about, much the same as when they choose an appropriate title for any other piece of writing. It also helps students learn the different parts of sending e-mail and using each one comfortably. A good title in the e-mail's subject window will help the recipient know what to expect the moment they get the child's message.
- Every letter we send and receive gives us more practice in the use of the polite letter form. We talk about the greeting: how to begin with a friendly comment to the reader, one that might start with a reference to previous mail our class received from that person, and perhaps some personal information about the sender or the recipient. The children learn to present the question itself only after we have taken care of these friendly formalities.
- Together, we work out the clearest way to ask the question the child has in mind. The question in anyone's head is more likely to get answered in a useful and understandable way when we do our best

to make that question very clear to the recipient. It may require some extended conversation and careful listening on my part before we arrive at what a child really wants to know or ask about. Whenever possible, we include the experience that generated the question the child is asking. This helps our correspondents know whether a child observed a bird doing something unusual during a walk near their house, found a mystery egg or nest on a hike, or that we've just finished reading a book about peregrine falcons living in cities. This restating of the context for the children's thinking helps reinforce us as active learners, both in the children's eyes and in those of our e-mail helpers. Sometimes a question may even be based on information we've gotten from another correspondent—and then we have intellectual cross-fertilization!

- I now include one other important piece of information with each child's question. This technique was first suggested in the following excerpt from a letter:

  > I'm curious what you think about why some birds have altricial babies and other birds have precocial babies. Maybe you could e-mail me some of your ideas, Petra. I'd be very interested in reading them.

  Because I've seen how much depth this step adds to our correspondence, I routinely ask a student to give her opinion or to make a guess about what the answer *might* be, before we send their question. Our research partners enjoy learning about the thinking our students are doing on their own. This shared theorizing puts the child in a very different role, as a co-scientist rather than just a passive recipient of information. Being able to see what the children themselves are thinking as they ask a question gives our correspondents something more to respond to when they reply, creates a dialogue rather than a lecture, and improves the quality of the answers we receive. Besides all these other benefits, taking time to ask students for their own theories about the questions they've raised gives me tremendous insights into how young children structure reality and try to make sense of their world. I enjoy seeing students begin to automaticaly include this step when they send an e-mail question.

- I routinely ask the children to type their own name at the end of their letter, as well as having them click the mouse to send their message on its way. This takes very little time and includes them in the conversational cycle of sending and receiving e-mail. It also improves their budding computer skills. Sometimes we'll walk over to the map at this point, to trace the approximate path of their message to the recipient.

Keeping Track of Mail You Send

I try to briefly write all questions on notebook paper as we send them. When we began using this approach midway through one year, I first asked the children to name all our correspondents and I wrote them, putting each research helper's name on one page. This was a terrific, though unintended, assessment of how aware the children were of our correspondents. Students were able to name fourteen of the fifteen people who wrote to us, without help from me. I was impressed, and so were they. I especially liked hearing the children refer to the people we wrote to as "the Hummingbird Guy," "the man who named his kids after birds," or "the one who took care of the raven." These associations demonstrated just how important each of these people's stories and lives really were to the children in our class.

Using the notebook or record pages is very simple. Each time a child sends e-mail to someone, you—or they—write on that correspondent's page the date, the child's name, and a very short summary of their question. This can tell you at a glance which correspondents are being sent the most mail, and which of your students are doing the most—or the least—writing. When an answer to that question arrives, you or the child checks it off, which gives you the further valuable information of which correspondents answer promptly and frequently. You can record the date the reply arrived if you want even more information.

This correspondence record is also a convenient place to have students briefly evaluate the answers they've received. You can have children record their reaction to the response in a variety of ways, depending on their age and interest. One year, we devised a rubric in the spring. The words and categories are from a brainstorm session, and are the children's suggestions.

Rubrics provide a way to evaluate something that's not usually quantifiable. Behavior, feelings, expectations, and performance can all be assessed using a rubric. After you've introduced your students to this concept, work with them to create and test their own rubrics about things they experience concretely. We practiced by making a list of reasonable behaviors while we were in the school library, which had been an issue with this particular group. Evaluating real behaviors with this framework makes it much easier for children to constructively evaluate the e-mails they receive. I want

Our email Research Rubric

① They didn't understand what I said.	① They sort of wrote a little bit about my question, but they didn't really understand it.	① They understood exactly what I wanted to know.
② I didn't think there was any information in their answer.	② Their answer is not as good as I expected it to be.	② They answered the question so it made sense.
③ They made my question get smaller.	③ I didn't get it, because they weren't thinking clearly enough to explain it well enough.	③ They made my question bigger.
		④ Their answer made me learn a lot, and it tempted me to keep writing back to them and asking questions.

April 22, 1997 brainstorm

The rubric was the result of a class discussion about the different kinds of answers the children were receiving, and it helped clarify their thinking about what they wanted from our research helpers when they sent an e-mail question.

my students to think back to what they expected to learn when they sent their question, and then compare it to the answer they received.

The point is not to "grade" the answers or to be critical of them, but rather for the children to assess what they have gained from each e-mail exchange. Do they feel the answer was a response to what they had been wondering about in the first place? Did it take them places they hadn't expected? Or are they still wondering about the initial question, for whatever reason—maybe because they have grown even more curious about the same topic?

This method of evaluating responses encourages children to take responsibility for their wondering and the learning that accompanies it. Rather than leaving the exchange at the very basic level of "I asked her something and she answered something," children are asked to look again at their question and the answer it generated. This leads them to appreciate a complete and articulate response even more, when they are able to see it in perspective. There's true conversation in these exchanges only when both participants are fully awake and aware; I do what I can to keep the children mindful of our share of the bargain.

Where Does It Fit? How Much Time Does It Take?

How best to engage children frequently in this form of research? Like much of life, it entails a combination of complex decisions and plain common sense. You'll probably want to give the research a predictable enough space in your classroom and your school day so that the children come to expect it as part of the curriculum. You will possibly need to monitor it—e-mail research can grow so huge that it's like zucchini plants in midsummer, threatening to take over your classroom entirely. Is it Language Arts? Social Studies? Science? You and your students will best be able to decide how e-mail inquiry fits into the school day and the rhythm of learning in your class.

Most of the children's questions seem to come up during our circle time at the rug, while we're reading or discussing a book on our topic, and from our experiences in and out of the classroom. It has been helpful to me to try to observe which parts of the day seem to work best for our

Internet research work. I can then plan our e-mail around these accessible times. Sending e-mail with a child who knows the routine can take just a few moments, so we sometimes manage to fit letters in during recess or a quick moment while the class is in transition.

Naturally, we do take occasional breaks from our topic, for example, during holiday celebrations, or when we're introducing new math units or other subjects, and when rehearsing and performing our rare class plays. And there are sometimes lulls when few e-mails arrive. Many times, these lulls simply stem from a lack of questions being sent out by us. In these cases, the children's enthusiasm for e-mail quickly returns just as soon as we restart the communications loop by sending out new questions to people. Their answers remind the children how great it feels to get mail, and then we are rolling once again.

You may occasionally find you are working with topics that just never seem to jell, or with groups of children who fail to reach previous levels of enthusiasm for using e-mail. It's important to be patient with the topic, the children, and your correspondents whenever a project seems to be moving slowly. It's amazing what just one outstanding e-mail reply can do to promote student interest in sending e-mail again! And remember that sending and receiving e-mail is an abstract concept for most of us, so allow plenty of time and experience for it to become a routine part of your class. It can sometimes take months of watching classmates sending and receiving e-mail in our class before some children realize they can participate.

It's important to recognize that this particular way of learning will naturally appeal more to—and make sense to—some children more than to others. It's possible to enjoy carrying out Internet research with the children who use it most readily, and not expect every child in your class to find it equally exciting as a means to gather information. You—and the most involved students—can share with the entire class most, if not all, of the letters that arrive. Hearing the correspondents' responses read aloud, much like a shared story or nonfiction book, allows everyone in your class to learn from and think about these e-mail exchanges. We can recognize that e-mail research may not personally appeal to every single child, while we encourage all of our students to enjoy the unique powers of this tool.

Chapter 8 Connections, Extensions, and Assessment

What's next? Having seen the power of e-mail research, you might want to consider what your students might do next with the information they've gained through their class research. You may be curious about how something as dynamic as student-led e-mail research can be assessed—and used for student assessment as well. What happens to your correspondents at the end of the year? And if you choose a new topic each year? Or you may have students whose families use the Internet at home and want to take advantage of this new means for conferencing and more. And finally, you might be wondering how to tap into the strengths of e-mail to improve your own teaching practice and stretch yourself professionally, using the Internet to build collaboration and support with teachers online.

Sharing E-mail Findings with Students' Work

What can be done to share or restate the information you and your students receive from your e-mail correspondents? Logical extensions of the e-mail research done by your class can come directly from your students, and the answers they receive can provide some interesting possible directions. Using the "I Am Wondering" project sheet can help guide children toward the next

steps in their thinking and learning. Sketches and brief writing done by younger students can combine very simply with the e-mail letters themselves, showing what was learned on a specific topic. More complex and long-term research projects can be created by combining information from a variety of resources, either by individuals or in teams formed from mutual interest in a topic.

Making a web page to share the children's research is an appealing possibility. If you're interested, you will want to enlist the help of someone experienced with website construction, or possibly read a book or take a class in web design. Many new software packages now exist that work just like word processors; these make simple web page creation much easier, yet still produce exciting, professional results. Older students can take an active part in the process, while younger ones can collaborate with you or another person skilled in website creation.

Students may choose to make graphs or create other visual displays of data to show the data they've collected. Surveys are quite easy to do with e-mail; using the computer's copy-and-paste tools to reproduce and customize similar messages, students can send the same request for information to many different recipients. One of my students wanted to find out which birds our correspondents had "right around their houses." He was pleased to discover how simple it was to send multiple queries. By sending repeated mailings of just his one question, this student was able to learn quite quickly about many of our correspondents' backyard birds around the world.

How Well Is It Working? And What Are They Learning?

Rudie Tretten and Peter Zachariou served as assessors of the Project-Based Learning Program supported by the Autodesk Foundation of Marin County. Their findings, based on extensive interviews with students, teachers, and parents, suggest that assessment of this kind, like the projects themselves, requires a variety of approaches and should take place over time in order to reflect what—as well as how—students are learning. Project-based learning isn't static and easily quantified. Traditional means of assessment, which rely on freezing a moment in time, usually in the form of a written test, aren't able to give a broad enough and realistic picture of ongoing student learning and behaviors in the context of project work.

To assess how well your project is working, you'll want to decide what your student outcomes actually are: Figure out what you're measuring before you reach for a yardstick! How are these outcomes—student mastery of the topic—linked with your district's standards for student achievement: competencies and skills that are measurable? What do you want students to learn from this immersion in a topic, and how can you be assured that they are truly absorbing critical information?

Teacher questions and ongoing observations are extremely helpful tools for evaluating what students are learning with this approach. I use a binder to store the anecdotal student observations I write throughout the school year. There is a separate section for each student, and I record behaviors, milestones, notes from phone or in-person parent conferences, goals, concerns, and strategies as often as possible. I can record student participation in e-mail research, noting when and how children demonstrate understanding or engagement in the process as well as the project.

Your e-mail research records and the "I Am Wondering" sheets will provide you with useful information about how children are participating in the class project or individual projects. And of course, culminating projects presented by students will demonstrate student learning and competencies clearly.

The following are some useful questions and ideas from Tretten and Zachariou's work:

- Can students articulate for outsiders and visitors what they are learning?
- Do students show an increased disposition to learn when using this approach?
- Do students view their learning as interconnected and interdisciplinary?
- Can students apply knowledge from one area, and make connections to new situations and information?
- Do students demonstrate understanding and mastery of the standards as well as the outcomes?

We can videotape students in action, over time, to document their level of engagement and understanding. These tapes can reveal new stages of awareness and competence in our students, and allow comparisons to be made throughout the year.

When using this approach to learning, student competencies may include the following skills and behaviors:

- making decisions regarding their chosen area of study (what resources to use, for example)
- participating in planning a project, whether working alone or with peers
- helping to establish rubrics for assessing the project or parts of the project
- solving problems that may occur during work on the project
- presenting findings or a summary of their work
- being able to think critically
- working in a focused and engaged manner
- using a variety of intelligences and honoring those in others
- thinking about thinking

Tretten and Zachariou caution that these assessments are necessary, but carry a risk: Student and teacher enthusiasm can be diminished or interfered with if we dissect something living in order to prove that it's working. We need to allow time for students and teachers to process what they—and we—are learning with this new approach. We need to blend responsible, outcome-based teaching and evaluations with engaged, student-led work.

Maintaining the Links with Your Research Helpers

We always thank our helpers at the end of each year—we want to be sure they know how much we appreciate their participation in our class. At the end of our very first year working with Internet helpers, I took a class photo to send to each of them. One child was holding a birder's photo album—a gift sent by two of our kindest correspondents—while other children were trying to hold a few of our newly hatched chicks. We mailed a copy of the picture, along with a thank-you card signed by the children, to each of the people who had faithfully written to us all year long. Other years, we have settled for sending a long letter of thanks, co-written by the children as a group project and e-mailed by the children. I also write personal letters to the people who have been our assistants, to thank them myself and also to let them know, when possible, what our research plans are for the next school year.

I don't like to repeat projects year after year. I want to approach a topic with fresh enthusiasm, and I want to leave the door open to student-generated project ideas, too. It's important that our correspondents understand why we're taking a break from the topic they assisted with, and that we'd like their help when we study that area again. I never want these wonderful people to feel taken for granted!

When we're beginning a new area of inquiry, I write to some of our previous research helpers. I ask if they feel skilled enough to field questions

We try to send a class photo and card of thanks to our e-mail helpers at the end of a year-long project.

on our new topic, or if they know of anyone else with expertise who might be able to help us. Graduate students are likely to know someone in a related field or discipline, and have often helped pass our request on to someone knowledgeable who is enthusiastic about helping with our new project.

Strengthening the School-Home Link Electronically

My options for communication with some parents have changed remarkably as more people have their own personal computers and Internet connections. Because several parents in my classes have e-mail at home, we often use it as a more immediate and less intrusive means of communication than phone calls, notes home, or conferences at school. It's been especially useful when children are ill and their parents need to let me know how long their child will be absent, or when they want to get assignments or class updates from me. Students can send instant electronic "get well" messages to sick classmates. Some children divide their time between two households, and can now exchange messages with the parent they aren't currently living with via the classroom computer. Sometimes a child will have a slump that affects their behavior or their progress at school; a short e-mail note sent home to the parents can immediately address the issue and help us compare notes. Before their child has arrived home that day, we can be already working cooperatively toward a solution. I also send e-mail notes home about a child's recent progress or a special breakthrough she has made. I like to include the child in this positive communication, so I try to compose the note with her help—or at least read it with her before I send it.

Probably my most interesting school-to-home computer communication was when a student from our school lived with his family for a year in Eastern Europe. Ordinarily, they lived in our town, and the boy had attended kindergarten in our school. However, he spent his first-grade year as an Independent Study Student in my class as a "virtual" first-grader. His parents communicated with me often by e-mail, describing their visits to castles and the differences in their city parks from our school playground, as well as sending questions and updates on his academic progress. I wrote in turn to them about what we were working on in class, and he occasionally even sent his homework assignments via e-mail. Phone calls were not possible, and surface mail took weeks to cross the Atlantic; e-mail allowed the children to communicate with him instantly—and cheaply enough to send him knock-knock jokes! The next year, he joined our class as a second-grader, and the children were eager to welcome him as someone whom they felt was already part of our class.

Examining Our Practice and Comparing Notes

Teacher collaboration by e-mail has been a fascinating gift for me, one that arose as a side venture from my initial bird project. While I was designing the bird research unit to include student e-mail research, I was also wondering a good deal—as I still am—about the ways in which other teachers allow for student input into their lives at school. I was curious about how science and other curricula can meet district and state requirements and yet still reflect students' interests. I was curious to learn how my colleagues handled this apparent conflict, so I sent out brief letters to that effect. I posted these in what I thought were likely places on the Internet. In addition to listservs for teachers, newsgroups beginning with "k12" offer a huge range of subtopics; you can choose an appropriate subgroup and post your message there, if theory and practice discussions interest you.

Three of the teachers who responded to my first posts have been writing ever since—some of us sporadically, and others regularly. Each of the teachers works in a setting unlike mine: One teaches older children, one teaches in an inner-city school, and the third works in a rural town the size of mine, but in the Midwest. It's entirely possible that if we four worked in the same school, we might not find much to talk about. However, online, we've been able to encourage each other through difficulties and offer suggestions, share enthusiasms, and describe new approaches that worked beautifully—or not the way we'd hoped. We compare our school administrations and even how we arrange our classrooms and schedule our days. We have all lent—and sometimes given—each other books, both professional books and those we read for pleasure.

Most important, we share with one another the selves behind the teachers we all are. We learn about each other's hobbies and ways we replenish ourselves. We can write about the exhaustion and frustration and self-doubt we feel—and joke about the whining that's sometimes unwise to inflict on the people we work side by side with daily, but that helps us regain a balance. I feel enriched by these relationships. I'm grateful to these e-pals, these research helpers of my own, for the chance they give me to regain perspective, share delight in success, and offer—as well as receive—ideas and direction, whenever our own fail us.

Another e-pal I write to almost daily works right in my school. Her classroom is a short walk down the hall from mine, but even when our classrooms were adjoined, we gleefully sent each other e-mails instead of calling through the wall or walking next door to talk. We've found there's something different, playful, and satisfying about composing your thoughts, seeing them on screen before sending them, that is part of the pleasure of communicating by e-mail. In addition to actual talk—we do visit each other's classrooms!—the two of us can also "talk" whenever it suits us by using e-mail, taking turns having bad days and encouraging each other.

I encourage you to consider finding colleagues with whom to correspond. You may not find the ideal correspondent right away. You might find people eager or able to write more often than you are, or you may enjoy writing in more detail than most people have time for. And then again, someone just might not appeal to you after you've exchanged a few notes. However, the benefits and pleasures of regular online colleague e-mail have, for me, far outweighed any inconveniences of a few false starts with others. I believe that e-mail correspondence will reward you with greatly enlarged views of teaching and the world and that it will vividly demonstrate for you its tremendous and unique power to bring together disparate people with shared enthusiasms.

Appendix

Observation Form

Name of scientist ______________ Date ______

I looked at ______________________

What I noticed: ______________

Some Common Country Codes

Zone	Country	Zone	Country
au	Australia	it	Italy
at	Austria	jp	Japan
be	Belgium	nl	The Netherlands
ca	Canada	no	Norway
cz	The Czech Republic	ru	The Russian Federation
dk	Denmark	es	Spain
fi	Finland	se	Sweden
fr	France	ch	Switzerland
de	Germany	tw	Taiwan
in	India	uk	The United Kingdom
ie	Ireland	us	The United States
il	Israel		

From Williams, *The Internet for Teachers*, p. 105

Some Useful Internet Addresses for Teachers

Be warned: addresses and resources on the Internet change with amazing speed!
You can e-mail the author at kidsonthenet@mcn.org

Directories

To search for newsgroups, websites, and listservs
http://www.dejanews.com

K–12 resource list of education-oriented newsgroups
http://edweb.gsn.org/usenets.html

Mailing list directory (listservs only)
http://www.liszt.com

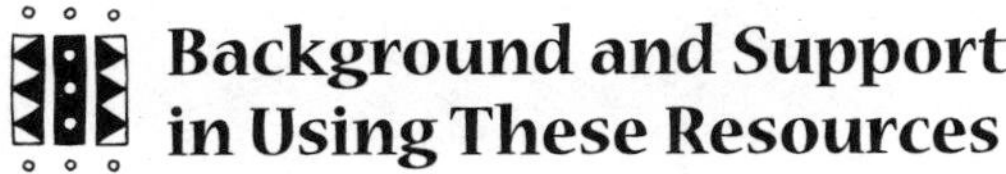

Background and Support in Using These Resources

Clear, helpful steps for using newsgroups
http://www1.iastate.edu/~hschmidt/newsgroups.html

Article about using the Web in education
http://edweb.sdsu.edu/edfirst/courses/web_ed.html

"Forum for K–12 Community to Read, Write, and Talk about Educational Technology"
http://www.gsh.org/wce/

Helpful article on Project-Based Learning
http://webgate.autodesk.com/foundation/resources/pubs/getreal.html

"What's on the Web? Sorting Strands of the World Wide Web for Educators," by Tom March, Pacific Bell Education First Fellow
http://edweb.sdsu.edu/edfirst/courses/webcue.html

Schoolnet Resource Manual has a huge number of Internet resources for education, and its directory includes basics like introductions to e-mail as well as netiquette tips.
ftp://schoolnet.carleton.capub/schoolnet/manuals/Resource.txt

"The Well Connected Educator" has articles, columns, and features about technology in education
http://www.gsh.org/wce/default.html

"Reinventing Schools" features thought-provoking ideas about technology in education
http://www.nap.edu/nap/online/techgap/

Newsgroups of special interest to educators are listed at this website:
http://edweb.gsn.org/usenets.html

The Projects Listserv can be reached at listserv@postoffice.cso.uiuc.edu

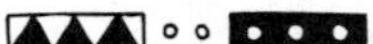

Bibliography

The Internet

Crumlish, C. 1997. *The Internet for Busy People*. 2d. ed. Berkeley, CA: Osborne/McGraw-Hill. (highly recommended)

Crumlish, C., and J. Hadfield. 1998. *Netscape Communicator for Busy People*. Berkeley, CA: Osborne.

Frazier, D., and B. Kurshan. 1995. *Internet for Kids*. rev. ed. Alameda, CA: Sybex.

James, P. *The Official Netscape Navigator Book*. Research Triangle Park, NC: Ventana Communications Group.

Maxwell, C., and C. Grycz. 1994. *New Riders' Official Internet Yellow Pages*. 2d ed. Indianapolis: New Riders.

Polly, J. 1997. *The Internet Kids and Family Yellow Pages*. 2d. ed. Berkeley, CA: Osborne/McGraw-Hill.

Williams, B. 1995. *The Internet for Teachers*. Foster City, IN: IDG Books Worldwide.

Birds—Student Resource Books and Stories

Alderton, D. 1993. *Nature Facts: Birds*. Surrey: CLB.

Amato, C., and D. Wenzel. 1996. *Penguins of the Galapagos*. Hauppauge, NY: Barron.

Arnold, C., and R. Hewett. 1991. *Flamingo.* New York: Morrow Junior Books.

Asch, F., and J. Marshall. 1978. *MacGooses' Grocery.* New York: Scholastic.

Atkinson, K. 1994. *Birds.* St. Leonards: Allen & Unwin.

Back, C., J. Olesen, and B. Jarner. 1992. *Chicken and Egg.* New York: Trumpet.

Baker, J. 1984. *Home in the Sky.* New York: Scholastic.

Bash, B. 1990. *Urban Roosts: Where Birds Nest in the City.* San Francisco: Sierra Club Books/Little, Brown.

Blake, Q. 1992. *Cockatoos.* New York: Trumpet Club/Little, Brown.

Bourgoing, P., and R. Mettler. 1992. *The Egg: A First Discovery Book.* New York: Scholastic.

Brighton, C. 1988. *Hope's Gift.* New York: Doubleday.

Burnie, D. 1993. *Eyewitness Books—Bird.* New York: Dorling-Kindersley.

Cohen, S., and G. Ellis. 1993. *Bird Nests.* San Francisco: Collins.

Cowley, J. 1994. *Hoiho's Chicks.* Katonah: Richard C. Owen.

Czernecki, S., and T. Rhodes. 1994. *The Hummingbird's Gift.* New York: Hyperion.

Delafosse, C., and R. Mettler. 1993. *Birds: A First Discovery Book.* New York: Cartwheel Books.

Doris, E., and L. Rubenstein. 1994. *Real Kids, Real Science: Ornithology.* New York: Thames Hudson.

Dunn, J. 1976. *The Little Duck.* New York: Random House.

Ehlert, L. 1993. *Feathers for Lunch.* New York: Harcourt Brace Jovanovich.

Flanagan, A. 1996. *Sea Birds.* New York: Children's Press.

Fox, M., and P. Mullins. 1987. *Hattie & the Fox.* New York: Trumpet.

Gans, R., and P. Mirocha. 1996. *How Do Birds Find Their Way?* New York: HarperCollins.

Garelick, M., and R. Jakobsen. 1975. *The Story of an Egg That Hatched: What's Inside?* New York: Scholastic.

Gill, P., et al. 1990. *Birds.* Mahwah, NJ: Troll.

Ginsburg, M., and B. Barton. 1980. *Good Morning, Chick.* New York: Scholastic.

Goldin, A., and L. Kessler. 1965. *Ducks Don't Get Wet.* New York: Thomas Crowell.

Haley, G. 1989. *Birdsong.* New York: Crown.

Harrell, B., and S. Roth. 1995. *How Thunder and Lightning Came to Be.* New York: Dial Books.

Harvey, O., and J. Wallace. 1985. *Blackbird's Nest.* Wellington: Learning Media.

Hornblow, L., and A. and M. Frith. 1965. *Birds Do the Strangest Things.* New York: Random House.

Jarrell, R. *The Bat-Poet.* 1967. Maurice Sendak. New York: MacMillan.

Jenkins, P., and M. Lloyd. 1996. *Falcons Nest on Skyscrapers.* New York: HarperCollins.

Johnston, T., and S. Garcia. n.d. *The Old Lady & the Birds.* New York: Harcourt Brace.

Krauss, R., and C. Johnson. 1967. *The Happy Egg.* New York: Scholastic.

Kwitz, M., and B. Degen. 1983. *Little Chick's Breakfast.* New York: Harper & Row.

Kwitz, M., and C. Szerkeres. 1978. *Little Chick's Story.* New York: Scholastic.

Lovett, S. 1992. *Extremely Weird Birds.* Santa Fe: John Muir.

McCauley, J. n.d. *Baby Birds and How They Grow.* Washington: National Geographic Society.

McCloskey, R. 1969. *Make Way for Ducklings.* New York: Scholastic.

McMillan, B. 1983. *Here a Chick, There a Chick.* New York: Trumpet.

McQueen, L. 1985. *The Little Red Hen.* New York: Scholastic.

Miller, M., and C. Nelson. 1989. *Talons: North American Birds of Prey.* Boulder: Johnson Books.

Mizumura, K. 1975. *The Emperor Penguins: Let's Read and Find Out.* London: Adam & Charles Black.

Oppenheim, J., and B. Reid. 1986. *Have You Seen Birds?* New York: Scholastic.

Oster, M. 1978. *The Illustrated Bird.* Garden City: Doubleday/Dolphin.

Parsons, A. 1990. *Eyewitness Juniors: Amazing Birds.* New York: Alfred A. Knopf.

Porter, K. 1986. *The Animal Kingdom: On the Wing.* Independence: Schoolhouse Press.

Rockwell, N. 1997. *Willie Was Different.* New York: Alfred A. Knopf.

Roy, R., and P. Galdone. 1979. *Three Ducks Went Wandering.* New York: Scholastic.

Serventy, V. 1983. *Animals in the Wild: Penguin.* New York: Scholastic.

Soper, T., and M. Loates. 1989. *Oceans of Birds.* London: David and Charles Publishers.

Stockley, C., et al. 1993. *Usborne Science and Nature: Ornithology.* Tulsa, OK: EDC.

Tafuri, N. 1984. *Have You Seen My Duckling?* New York: Scholastic/William Morrow.

Taylor, B. 1995. *Birds.* New York: Dorling-Kindersley Ltd.

Turkle, B. 1988. *Thy Friend, Obadiah.* New York: Trumpet/Viking Penguin.

Turner, A., and L. Desimini. 1989. *Heron Street.* New York: Scholastic.

Vessel, M., et al. 1967. *Introducing Our Western Birds: California State Series.* Sacramento: California State Department of Education.

Watts, B. 1987. *Birds' Nest.* Englewood Cliffs, NJ: Silver Burdett Press.

Wexo, J. 1994. *Ostriches & Other Ratites.* San Diego: Wildlife Education Ltd.

———. 1980. *Birds of Prey: ZooBooks.* San Diego: Wildlife Education Ltd.

Wolff, A. 1988. *A Year of Birds.* New York: Puffin Books.

Adult Reference Books—Birds

Doris, E. 1991. *Doing What Scientists Do: Children Learn to Investigate Their World.* Portsmouth, NH: Heinemann.

Dunn, J., E. Blom, et al. 1996. *Field Guide to the Birds of North America.* 2d ed. Washington: National Geographic Society.

Dunning, J. 1994. *Secrets of the Nest: The Family Life of North American Birds.* New York: Houghton Mifflin.

Ehrlich, P., D. Dobkin, and D. Wheye. 1988. *The Birder's Handbook.* New York: Simon & Schuster/Fireside Books.

Hiller, I. 1989. *Introducing Birds to Young Naturalists.* College Station: Texas A&M University Press.

Kastner, J. 1985. *A World of Watchers.* San Francisco: Sierra Club/Knopf.

Naturescope, National Wildlife Federation. *Birds, Birds, Birds!* Washington, D.C.

Pasquier, R., and M. LaFarge. 1977. *Watching Birds.* Boston: Houghton Mifflin.

Stokes, D., and L. Stokes. 1996. *Stokes Field Guide to Birds.* Boston: Little, Brown.

Terres, J. 1994. *Songbirds in Your Garden.* Chapel Hill, NC: Algonquin Books.

Udvardy, M., and J. Farrand. 1997. *National Audubon Society Field Guide to North American Birds, Western Region.* New York: Chanticleer Press.

CD-ROMS

The Multimedia Bird Book (Workman/Swifte)

Eyewitness Virtual Reality Bird (Eyewitness)

National Audubon Society Interactive CD-ROM Guide to North American Birds (C-Wave)